Higher Education Leadership:
Enhancing Skills through Professional
Development Programs

by Sharon A. McDade

ASHE-ERIC Higher Education Report No. 5, 1987

Prepared by

 Clearinghouse on Higher Education
The George Washington University

Published by

 Association for the Study of
Higher Education

Jonathan D. Fife,
Series Editor

Cite as
McDade, Sharon A. *Higher Education Leadership: Enhancing Skills through Professional Development Programs.* ASHE-ERIC Higher Education Report No. 5. Washington, D.C.: Association for the Study of Higher Education, 1987.

Managing Editor: Christopher Rigaux
Manuscript Editor: Sharon Block/Block Communications

The ERIC Clearinghouse on Higher Education invites individuals to submit proposals for writing monographs for the Higher Education Report series. Proposals must include:
1. A detailed manuscript proposal of not more than five pages.
2. A chapter-by-chapter outline.
3. A 75-word summary to be used by several review committees for the initial screening and rating of each proposal.
4. A vita.
5. A writing sample.

Library of Congress Catalog Card Number 88-70150
ISSN 0884-0040
ISBN 0-913317-40-3

Cover design by Michael David Brown, Rockville, Maryland

ERIC Clearinghouse on Higher Education
School of Education and Human Development
The George Washington University
One Dupont Circle, Suite 630
Washington, D.C. 20036-1183

ASHE Association for the Study of Higher Education
Texas A&M University
Department of Educational Administration
Harrington Education Center
College Station, Texas 77843

This publication was prepared partially with funding from the Office of Educational Research and Improvement, U.S. Department of Education, under contract no. 400-86-0017. The opinions expressed in this report do not necessarily reflect the positions or policies of OERI or the Department.

EXECUTIVE SUMMARY

American higher education continues to face difficult times. As the number of problems has grown over the past decades, the many constituencies of the higher education enterprise have searched for stronger managers and visionary leaders. It is not enough to be only an administrator or only a leader. Colleges and universities need leaders and managers who can turn their visions into reality (Birnbaum 1983; Keller 1983; Dressel 1981; Rausch 1980).

Since many senior academic administrators of colleges and universities first trained for academic careers in research and teaching and scarcely anticipated their current administrative positions, they have had minimal management training. Both academic and nonacademic officers with years of administrative experience find that they must quickly develop the new and different knowledge and skills needed to manage an institution when they move into senior leadership positions. Likewise, administrators in senior positions must continue to grow as leaders while adapting to a constantly changing environment (Kerr 1984; Keller 1983; Rausch 1980; Gaff et al. 1978; Scott 1978a, 1978b; Fisher 1977; Henderson 1970).

Although on-the-job training is best, mistakes can be costly to individuals and institutions. Reading is probably the most common way to acquire knowledge about management and leadership, but it is a passive learning mode. Professional development programs provide a more active alternative: They increase knowledge, add to and enhance management skills and leadership techniques, broaden perspectives, and stimulate creativity.

While many administrators enthusiastically embrace professional development programs, other administrators just as actively ignore them. Although such programs have existed in higher education almost as long as they have in business and industry, they have never achieved the same acceptance in education (Green 1987; Keller 1983; Fisher 1978; Higher Education Management Institute 1978; Scott 1978a, 1978b). A more complete understanding of the types and benefits of professional development programs as well as their problems and drawbacks may enable executives to take advantage of these programs as learning experiences.

For this investigation, a senior administrator is defined as a president or an officer who reports directly to the president, supervises a major division of the institution, and has substantive policy-setting responsibilities. A middle-level administrator manages a major enterprise within the academy and charts a future for that unit within the broad policy map established by the senior executive team. Professional development (including both management and leadership development) denotes programs that "increase the capacity of individuals to provide leadership, to be effective in their work and thereby improve the effectiveness and the quality of a college or university" (Green 1987, p. 1).

What Career Paths Lead to Administration?

It is necessary to identify various career paths to discern fully the development needs of administrators and to understand the reluctance of many to participate extensively in these programs. Many academic administrators began their careers as faculty members. Yet the department chair, the most common entry position into academic administration, has not been the first step of the majority. In addition to the traditional ladder—department chair, dean, provost, and president—other paths are now just as common, including assorted entry-level positions within higher education institutions and in related areas of secondary education and education agencies and organizations. Nonacademic administrators enter administration and rise through the ranks through another set of varied paths.

Because administrators follow many career paths, their skills, knowledge, and expertise depend on their experiences. For every administrative and leadership strength developed and polished through on-the-job experience, just as many weaknesses are ignored because of lack of opportunity, time, or assessment.

What Skills and Knowledge Are Required For Executive Positions?

To understand the significance of professional development to all administrators, it is important to understand their responsibilities. In any consideration of administrative responsibilities, it is impossible to separate leadership and administrative responsibilities, since most leaders also must manage and most managers must occasionally lead (Gardner 1986).

Administrators, particularly senior executives, are responsible for developing visions and goals and for achieving them. Although others may actually run the systems and tend the processes, the senior officers are ultimately responsible for the operations that enable the complex enterprise of the modern college or university to function. The senior officers are responsible for the interrelationship between the environment and the institution. They must develop people, a working climate, and good communications (Gardner 1986; Bennis 1984; Kerr 1984; Whetten 1984; Birnbaum 1983; Keller 1983; Blyn and Zoerner 1982; Kauffman 1982; Blake et al. 1981; Campanella et al. 1981).

In surveys of business, government, and secondary and higher education, administrators indicated that organization and planning skills were the most important, while human skills ranked second and financial management and control third (McDonough-Rogers et al. 1982a, 1982b; Digman 1980; Lutz and Ferrante 1972).

What Lessons about Professional Development Can Be Gained from Other Fields?
Professional development for all management levels is accepted in business, industry, the military, and government. Business alone spends nearly $60 billion each year on professional development, with a significant percentage of that sum going to programs for senior administrators (Green 1987; Ingols 1986; Eurich 1985; Sonnenfeld 1983). Although colleges and universities offer the most prestigious of these executive programs, corporations have begun to compete with offerings from in-house institutes (Gardner 1987; Fresina 1986; Sonnenfeld 1983; Lusterman 1977).

What Programs Are Available to Administrators?
Different types of programs are available for professional development: national institutes and internships; administrative conferences; conventions; and meetings, seminars, and workshops.

What Are the Benefits and Problems of Participation?
Although the benefits of participating in professional development programs are easy to identify, value is difficult to quantify. Participants provide strong anecdotal evidence of the personal worth of those programs, but no comprehensive studies have surveyed several programs to collect quantitative evidence of benefits.

The knowledge derived from the curriculum is the most obvious benefit. Other benefits—less easily identifiable and described but no less important—include new ideas, stimulation, contacts and networking, access to reference materials, team building, time for reflection and thought, increased promotability, increased access to senior positions for women and minorities, opportunities to augment previous experience through simulation instead of through costly on-the-job mistakes, improved specialization, broadened perspectives, and increased self-confidence (Green *Forthcoming*; Gardner 1987; Argyris and Cyert 1980; Starcevich and Sykes 1980; Godsey 1983; Green 1983; Eble 1978; Kanter and Wheatley 1978; Levinson 1968; Andrews 1966). Although the little evidence that exists only documents some of these benefits (for example, promotability and access), the myths surrounding some are pervasive and can become self-fulfilling prophecies.

These benefits must always be balanced against the drawbacks of participation, including career timing, the obsolescence of training, the costs in time and money, and the issues of selection, integration, evaluation, and feedback (Gardner 1987; McDade 1986; Hodgkinson 1981; Lindquist 1981; Kanter and Wheatley 1978).

What Professional Development Issues Face Higher Education Administrators?

The evidence that does exist on the benefits—anecdotal, tentative, and personal as it may be—still outweighs the disadvantages for many administrators. The issue is then how to use professional development programs so that administrators and institutions can derive the greatest benefit. A fully integrated and dynamic plan requires the commitment not only of the executive participants but also of an institution's trustees.

To be most effective, professional development experiences need to be part of an integrated, comprehensive organizational plan that links development activities with the actual tasks and responsibilities of the job. Improved preparation can help participants absorb the experience with clear expectations about how the new information or skills will later be used. While much research on such related areas as adult development and learning styles already exists, further research is still needed on management and leadership development. Foundations can continue to affect the leadership of colleges and universities by investing in professional development for administrators in a variety of ways.

ADVISORY BOARD

Roger G. Baldwin
Assistant Professor of Education
College of William and Mary

Carol M. Boyer
Senior Policy Analyst for Higher Education
Education Commission of the States

Clifton F. Conrad
Professor of Higher Education
Department of Educational Administration
University of Wisconsin–Madison

Elaine H. El-Khawas
Vice President
Policy Analysis and Research
American Council on Education

Martin Finkelstein
Associate Professor of Higher Education Administration
Seton Hall University

Carol Everly Floyd
Associate Vice Chancellor for Academic Affairs
Board of Regents of the Regency Universities System
State of Illinois

George D. Kuh
Associate Dean for Academic Affairs
School of Education
Indiana University

Yvonna S. Lincoln
Associate Professor of Higher Education
University of Kansas

Richard F. Wilson
Assistant to the Chancellor
University of Illinois

Ami Zusman
Principal Analyst, Academic Affairs
University of California

CONSULTING EDITORS

Paul A. Albrecht
Executive Vice President and Dean
Claremont Graduate School

Harriet W. Cabell
Associate Dean for Adult Education
Director, External Degree Program
University of Alabama

L. Leon Campbell
Provost and Vice President for Academic Affairs
University of Delaware

Roderick S. French
Vice President for Academic Affairs
George Washington University

Timothy Gallineau
Vice President for Student Development
Saint Bonaventure University

Madeleine F. Green
Director, Center for Leadership Development
American Council on Education

Milton Greenberg
Provost
American University

Margaret Heim
Senior Research Officer
Teachers Insurance and Annuity Association/College
  Retirement Equity Fund

Frederic Jacobs
Dean of the Faculties
American University

Hans H. Jenny
Executive Vice President
Chapman College

Joseph Katz
Director, New Jersey Master Faculty Program
Woodrow Wilson National Fellowship Foundation

L. Lee Knefelkamp
Dean, School of Education
American University

David A. Kolb
Professor and Chairman
Department of Organizational Behavior
The Weatherhead School of Management
Case Western Reserve University

Jules B. LaPidus
President
Council of Graduate Schools in the United States

Judith B. McLaughlin
Research Associate on Education and Sociology
Harvard University

Theodore J. Marchese
Vice President
American Association for Higher Education

John D. Marshall
Assistant to the Executive Vice President and Provost
Georgia State University

Sheila A. Murdick
Director, National Program on Noncollegiate-Sponsored
  Instruction
New York State Board of Regents

Steven G. Olswang
Assistant Provost for Academic Affairs
University of Washington

Thomas J. Quatroche
Professor and Chair, Educational Foundations Department
State University College at Buffalo

S. Andrew Schaffer
Vice President and General Counsel
New York University

Henry A. Spille
Director, Office on Educational Credits and Credentials
American Council on Education

CONTENTS

FOREWORD

There is no professional area in our society where advanced training or formal education is less accepted than in the area of higher education administration. This is true at all levels, from the president to the department chair. For the president, the three most common backgrounds are: 1) faculty experience in an academic discipline; 2) law; and 3) the ministry. For department chairs, usually the first academic administrative post attained, more often than not the first prerequisite is willingness to take on the position, and second, academic expertise. Normally administrative training or background is not considered.

Considering that higher education is a nearly $100 billion industry, equalling roughly 4% of the gross national product, this lack of credibility given to administrative training seems appalling. It would be equally appalling, however, to discount the importance that academic training and experience plays in the background of successful college administrators. It is becoming apparent that as the management of colleges and universities becomes more sophisticated and competitive, the need for personnel with a balance between academic and management training will be more evident.

Due to this need, the number of professional development programs is increasing. Through them, institutions can improve management skills of their administrators without major organizational disruptions. Developing a coordinated strategy that promotes professional development at all levels of the institution sends a message that not only are both academic experience and management skills valued, but also that the experiences of other institutions that are part of most professional development programs, have value. Professional development programs have the added benefit of widening the network of contacts available for professional advice-giving.

This report by Sharon McDade, director of the Institute for Educational Management at Harvard University, is useful on several levels. First, she traces the typical career paths of administrators, showing what skills they typically gain through on-the-job training and other sources. Then she discusses what skills and knowledge are most necessary, based in part on similar positions outside of academe. She next surveys the different programs available nationwide, eliciting their strengths and weaknesses. Finally, she makes a number of recommendations for implementing a cohesive on-campus program to coordinate overall staff development, from middle-managers to institutional leaders.

As we enter the 21st century, higher education can no longer solely depend on on-the-job training to develop its institutional leaders. Only the best-managed institutions will be able to get the most from limited resources. Colleges and universities that take concerted care in the professional development of their personnel will be the ones to flourish. This report will be highly useful for institutions who wish to establish a strategy for campus-wide professional development.

Jonathan D. Fife
Professor and Director
ERIC Clearinghouse on Higher Education
School of Education and Human Development
The George Washington University

CAREER PATHS TO ADMINISTRATION

One way to investigate and understand the professional development habits and needs of college and university administrators is to understand their career paths. Although the hierarchy of the academy may appear to outside observers to be very regularized, there is actually great variety in the career ladders leading to the senior levels of administration. Research on career paths tends to divide this variety into academic and non-academic administrators.

In a study of the theoretical approaches to the study of the careers of higher education administrators, Twombly (1986b) noted that career mobility in colleges and universities follows four models: through positions at the same institution with greater status and responsibility, through evolving jobs at the same institution that often involve different titles, through departure from one institution for a higher position at another institution, and through acceptance of a lower position at an institution that has higher status. This differs from the well-defined ladder of career-building experiences and positions often found in business, industry, or the military. The nonacademic positions (chief business officers, chief student affairs officers, chief institutional advancement officers) appear to be ceiling positions, as none provide significant numbers of presidents. While there may be horizontal movement across these career lines at the lower levels, there is virtually no horizontal movement at the senior levels.

Higher education follows a pattern of natural selection with little planning or preparation by the individual or the organization for the leadership of the future.

Career Paths for Academic Administrators

Tradition holds that academic administrators rise from faculty ranks and follow a path from professor to department chair to dean, provost, and eventually president. While business and industry have found it important to identify and groom future leaders through career and succession planning, higher education follows a pattern of natural selection with little planning or preparation by the individual or the organization for the leadership of the future (Moore 1983; Moore et al. 1983).

Four recent studies have been conducted on the careers of academic administrators. The "Leaders in Transition" study by Moore and associates is the largest and most comprehensive. This 1981 study of 4,000 academic line administrators in four-year colleges and universities attempted to categorize the steps to the positions of academic dean and president (Moore 1984, 1983; Moore and Sagaria 1982; Moore et al. 1983). In 1984, Moore and associates conducted a similar study of the senior (academic and nonacademic) administrators of community and two-year institutions (Twombly 1986a, 1986b; Moore et al 1985). A study by D. J. Socolow, then a visiting research fellow at the National Institute of Education, examined career paths followed by presidential candidates responding to advertisements in the *Chronicle of Higher Education* during a specific period (1978). A fourth study by Paul S. Poskozim, a professor at Northeastern Illinois University in Chicago, explored all administrative moves posted in the "Gazette" section of the *Chronicle* for the academic year 1982–83 (1984). Although these studies focused primarily on the career paths of presidents and deans, their results can be generalized to other academic administrators. When they can provide illuminating detail, other less recent or comprehensive studies will be noted also.

Professorial roots
The findings from these studies are similar and complementary. The major discovery made by all four and reinforced by other available research supports the commonly held belief that the careers of the majority of academic line and staff administrators are rooted in the professoriat (Twombly 1986a, 1986b; Kerr 1984; Moore et al. 1983; Ironside 1983, 1981; Fullerton and Ellner 1978; Socolow 1978). Not much has changed since 1978, when Eble found that "eight out of ten [presidents] have had college teaching experience" (p. 91; Twombly 1986a, 1986b; Allen 1984; Moore 1984; Ironside 1983, 1981; Fullerton and Ellner 1978).

While citing the common roots in the professoriat, James L. Fisher, in his book on power and college presidents, noted that although most presidents may have had faculty experience, these roots may not be as deep as many have thought: "Effective presidents were generally younger (early forties rather than fifties), had taught fewer years (fewer than five rather than more than ten), had a stronger sense of mission, and were not necessarily educated in a traditional academic discipline" (1984, p. 23). Moore and her associates determined that a "fairly large percentage of individuals (19 percent for presidents, 15 percent for academic deans) have managed to reach their current positions without faculty experience" (Moore et al. 1983, p. 514).

Tradition has it that the ladder of common steps between professor and president includes department chair, dean, and provost. Instead, Moore found that

> *The normative presidential career trajectory is accurate only to the extent that permutations and variations among its elements are incorporated. As a strictly defined, hierarchical, linear model, it does not reflect the actual experience of a national sample of current college and university presidents. It is most accurate in describing the principal entry portal to the college presidency—faculty experience—and to identify four other positions that commonly appear within the trajectory, of which the provost position seems the most potent for predicting a subsequent move to a presidency. The academic deanship and the department chairmen are less common elements in the route to a presidency. Other administrative positions within an institutional context appear to be common substitutes for these two positions* (Moore et al. 1983, p. 513).

In all, Moore and her associates established that only 3.2 percent of the presidents surveyed followed the traditional ladder. In comparison, 32.1 percent of the presidents had skipped as many as three positions on the traditional ladder. According to Moore, "more individuals conform to the variations from the 'norms' than to the 'norms' themselves" (1983, p. 5). Poskozim found that, while 85 percent of the new presidents in his study had previously held at least one of the ladder positions, the other 15 percent mainly came from outside academe—government agencies and various state and federal education agencies—and had held none of the ladder positions (Poskozim 1984, p. 57).

The department chair
Traditionally, the position of department chair has been considered the most common point of entry into administration. But Moore and associates discovered that this was "the least potent rung" in provosts' and presidents' career paths. Other kinds of administrative experiences "are most often substituted" for the department chair position (Moore et al. 1983, p. 514; Moore 1984). In their study of the career paths of chief officers of graduate education, Fullerton and Ellner found that only half of their sample of 102 administrators had chaired a department; rather, positions such as assistant or associate dean and nonacademic positions substituted for this experience (1978).

J. H. L. Roach, in a study of department chairs, found that while this position was the most common entry point into academic administration, as the size of the institution increased other "subordinate administrative jobs within a department or division may precede chairing a department or directing a division" (Eble 1978, p. 4). Twombly found that in two-year institutions, it was just as common to hold a first management position as it was to chair a department. These other positions are also springboards to higher administrative positions, even though Moore and Sagaria found that "movement from a staff position to a line position is atypical" (1982, p. 511).

The study by Moore and her associates on the career paths of academic deans showed that "fewer variations on the posited trajectory are required to encompass the majority of deans' experiences" (1983, p. 513). While most deans rose from the faculty, 20 percent came from outside the professoriat, although their experiences tended to be in areas strongly associated with education. Outsiders tended to enter as assistant or associate deans before moving into deanships. Poskozim found that "one out of every three newly appointed deans (or about 35 percent) came from the professoriat, 20 percent, or the largest single source, directly from the home institution" (1984, p. 56).

In addition, Moore and her associates discovered that deans of professional schools were most likely to come directly from the faculty, while deans of arts and sciences divisions and graduate schools more typically (42 percent) had spent time as a department chair. A 1980 profile compiled by G. D. Hadley and R. W. Warren indicated that the typical new business school dean had "taught [at] between five and nine schools, was appointed to his first deanship at a school where he had been teaching as a full professor, had been a department head for about four years, had written no books, and published fewer than five journal articles" (Blyn and Zoerner 1982, p. 23).

Career Paths for Nonacademic Administrators
A large group of administrators supports the higher education enterprise in middle-level and senior positions but is not in the academic line. These nonacademic managers often have graduate training, years of experience, and administrative expertise similar to that of their academic manager associates (Moore and Sagaria 1982; Scott 1978b).

Entry positions

The great variety among these first management positions of nonacademic administrators makes categorization difficult. While no single position or type of position was, by itself, the most common first position, entry-level staff and line management positions combined constituted the most common first experience. Although it is most common for chief student affairs officers to begin in student affairs areas such as counseling and residence hall management and for chief institutional advancement officers to begin on fund-raising or alumni affairs staffs, there is also evidence of horizontal movement from one area to another at the entry level.

The faculty was also a significant source for nonacademic administrators, second only to the combined count of entry-level management positions (Twombly 1986a, 1986b; Moore et al. 1985; Rickard 1985; Ostroth et al. 1984; Harder 1983; Moore and Sagaria 1982). For example, more than half of the chief student affairs officers have had teaching experience (Ostroth et al. 1984; Moore and Young 1987).

The third most common first position for nonacademic officers was outside higher education. Ostroth, Efird, and Lerman reported that 30 percent of the chief student affairs officers in their survey "started their careers in elementary or secondary education, 9 percent in religious service, 8 percent in the military, and 7 percent in business" (1984, p. 444). Harder found that 39 percent of her sample of chief student affairs officers began as public school teachers or coaches (1983, p. 444). Twombly noted that a high proportion of chief business officers moved directly to their current positions from business and industry and school administration (1986a, 1986b). Ironside discovered that more women than men "most often began with school teaching, followed by some graduate work which led to college-level teaching and then administration" (1983, p. 15).

Career experiences

Like academic administrators, nonacademic administrators build careers in several ways. Surveys of the career paths of nonacademic administrators indicated that while upward movement at the same institution may be possible in the entry- and middle-level positions, most administrators must move to another institution to make a substantial jump into an upper-middle or lower-senior position. However, most senior nonacademic officers moved into their current position from a previous position in the same institution (Moore 1984; Twombly 1986a, 1986b; Rickard 1985; Ostroth et al. 1984; Harder 1983). On average, chief student affairs officers worked at only two positions before moving into their current senior position (Ostroth et al. 1984; Harder 1983). A third of these senior officers began "their student affairs careers in executive positions, although the average administrator was in the profession at least six years before becoming the chief student affairs person" (Moore and Young 1987, p. 7). Business officers at two-year institutions most commonly entered a senior position directly from outside higher education (Twombly 1986a).

Nonacademic administrators have published very little. Ostroth, Efrid, and Lerman found that, while approximately 27 percent of the chief student affairs officers in their sample have had at least one national publication, only 8 percent have had more than three national publications (1984, p. 444).

Interpretations of the Studies
The details of these studies can be summarized and generalized. True to tradition, the vast majority of academic and nonacademic administrators began their careers as teachers in either elementary, secondary, or higher education. The bulk of those who did not come from the professoriat had some type of related educational experience (school administration, educational agencies, and organizations). Except for business officers, few university administrators have worked in business and industry.

The department chair, while the single most common entry position into academic administration, has not been the path of the majority of academic officers. Although the traditional ladder to senior-level academic management from department chair, dean, provost, and president is still valid, other paths through academic administration and, although numbers are still very small, through student affairs, finance and administration, alumni affairs, and institutional advancement are increasingly cited. Career ladders to senior positions in nonacademic areas are even more vague and contain greater variety. Thus, there is more mobility from staff to line nonacademic positions than there is in academic administration. Nonacademic administrators can acquire managerial experience in a broader variety of positions and experiences.

In the upward mobility of both academic and nonacademic administrators, some of the traditional hierarchy rungs are often skipped entirely. In many cases, a person may hold several positions on one rung, usually in successively larger institutions, and then jump several rungs. Most academic and nonacademic administrators had at least some prior administrative experience before moving into the senior ranks. According to Poskozim, almost 20 percent prepared for a presidency by serving in a previous presidency (1984, p. 59). A quarter of chief student affairs officers had served in the same position at another institution before moving to their current institution (Rickard 1985; Ostroth et al. 1984). On average, both academic and nonacademic senior administrators remain in a position from four to seven and one-half years (Twombly 1986a, 1986b; Harder 1983; Ostroth et al. 1984; Moore 1984; Lunsford 1984).

A substantial number of administrators moved into senior positions at their institutions (Moore et al 1985; Lunsford 1984). In her study of four-year institutions, Moore found that "over 65 percent of the line administrators we surveyed had held at least one previous job or had earned at least one of their degrees from the institution in which they currently work" (1984).

In two-year institutions, Moore discovered that presidents and campus executives had the highest rate of participation in external professional development activities. Chief business officers participated in the fewest development activities and reported that they were not important to their career advancement. While chief student affairs officers also were not highly likely to participate in external fellowships, internships, and management institutes, they were more likely to attend specialized workshops in student affairs and to feel that participation in such workshops was important to their careers.

There is remarkably little variation among the groups of administrators . . .concerning the types of external activities in which they participate, but there is considerable variation in the degree to which each type participates. On the whole, the three most popular external activities are: boards of directors of state or regional professional associations, external consulting, and publication activities. The topmost administrators—presidents and campus executives—tend to participate most extensively and in a broader range of activities (Moore 1984, p. 49).

Academic administrators in all types of institutions are more likely to have retained active links with their academic discipline and scholarly backgrounds. They continue membership in academic organizations, occasionally present scholarly papers at conventions, and may even hold positions as officers in these discipline associations (McDade 1986; Williams 1986; Allen 1984).

Implications for Professional Development
The unique and highly individualized career paths of higher education administrators pose special needs and distinctive challenges for administrative maturation and management team building. In many businesses and in the military, career progress is rather uniform. Administrators and officers progress through a series of job levels, each with known challenges and experiences. Generals and company executives alike know that their officers or administrators have had comparable experiences and developed similar skills and capabilities. There is a common base from which to build an effective and efficient management team. Administrators and officers attend professional development programs at regular intervals and study a prescribed, organized curriculum to develop specified skills and to prepare for predicted next challenges.

In higher education, career progress is highly individualized, erratic, and circumstantial. While this variety of experiences provides a richness of outlook, there is no common base of skills and abilities. Unlike business, industry, government, and the military—where professional development is an accepted, normal way to build skills and enhance abilities—higher education prefers experiential learning. For all administrators, academic and nonacademic alike, professional development is an underused tool and opportunity.

At the most basic level, professional development activities fulfill an acculturation role for those who did not hold faculty positions or for those who skipped certain experiences during earlier parts of their careers. Although many members of the academy insist that administrators need faculty experience to be able to understand their environment completely, Eble saw it as a point of concern that could be addressed through professional development. "Certainly education is a distinctive and important enough enterprise that its administrators should have experience with academic matters. Yet the range of selection may stand in the way of developing and making use of administrative talent outside the professoriate" (1978, p. 91). Eble believed the academy was narrowing its opportunities for leadership by relying so heavily on its own members instead of allowing occasional infusions of new blood to enrich the leadership stock. Administrators without faculty experience can deepen their understanding of the purposes, culture, and problems of higher education through participation in professional development experiences.

From her studies of the patterns of administrative career paths in higher education, Moore provided another implication for professional development. She compared administrators who build an "occupational career" of more challenging and higher-level positions in a number of institutions with those who fill a succession of positions in mainly one institution. She found that an external candidate who fills a position brings new management talent to an institution, but those skills and expertise were developed at the expense of another institution. Therefore, when an administrator leaves one institution for another, the first school loses the benefit of the inside culture and organizational knowledge gained by that administrator over years of experience. The new administrator will need months, if not years, to acquire the same knowledge. In the long run, it may be cheaper and wiser to provide professional development to enhance the management skills and leadership abilities of current administrators rather than to bring in outsiders to fill administrative positions.

Administrators who spend their entire careers in one or two institutions need professional development opportunities for other reasons. Such executives need to go outside their institutions to refine their management and leadership talents, and professional development programs, in particular, provide a vehicle for this training.

Harold Hodgkinson, a higher education researcher and writer who focuses on adult education and development, derived yet another view concerning professional development for higher education administrators. He noted that while professors generally move into their careers directly from graduate school, administrators come to their roles considerably later in life. Faculty usually received direct training for their teaching and research roles during their years in graduate school.

Few administrators receive the same kind of direct training to be administrators as professors did. In addition, Hodgkinson noted, "one often has to muck around in the [administrative] role for a while to find out whether or not it is compatible'' before committing oneself to administration as a career (1981, p. 725). Because of this late entry and the many paths taken to enter administration, it is difficult for institutions to organize a system for administrative preparation. Instead, executives are left on their own to develop administrative and leadership talents in whatever way possible. What was not learned before moving into an administrative position has to be learned afterward, either through on-the-job training or through professional development.

Summary
In summary, although some patterns of career paths to senior academic and nonacademic positions are discernible, the very variety of these paths ensures that administrators at any particular level in an institution will not have comparable work experiences, leadership abilities, and administrative capabilities. While this diversity adds a richness of outlook and variety of talents to an institution's administration, it also brings an unevenness with unexpected weaknesses. Producing the best administrative leadership from such a disparate group of managers can be an insurmountable challenge. Professional development activities and programs provide an important mechanism for augmenting experiences, strengthening weaknesses, and providing the background that can make the difference in the creation of a truly effective administrative team.

SKILLS AND KNOWLEDGE NECESSARY FOR ADMINISTRATION

Responsibilities of Administrators

To understand how professional development can aid administrators, it is first necessary to know what administrators do and for what they are responsible. There is rich discussion on these topics in the leadership and management literature, especially as they pertain to senior executives. Virtually everyone who has written a book in these areas has included a section on roles, responsibilities, and skills. While many of the lists overlap, some are unique and add interesting insights.

Many authors try to distinguish between leadership and management.[1] Despite these efforts, the resulting definitions all ultimately refer to the responsibility for directing an organization's vision and resources toward achieving the greatest results (Drucker 1973). While some believe these words have specific and distinct meanings, in practice they are too closely intertwined for significant differentiation since "most managers exhibit some leadership skills, and most leaders on occasion find themselves managing" (Gardner 1986, p. 13). College and university administrators must be both leaders and managers if they wish to accomplish the goals of their institutions and build for the future.

In the higher education literature of leadership and administration, most discussions focus on the responsibilities of the president and academic dean. However, this information can be generalized for academic and nonacademic administrators and for all levels of administrators of colleges and universities. In the complex enterprises that modern colleges and universities have become, the responsibility for leadership resides not only with the president, but with the other administrators in an executive team. This responsibility is interpreted for implementation by middle-level administrators.

The following list summarizes the most often cited responsibilities of administrators. This list, while interesting because it breaks down an administrator's activities for better examination and understanding, could also serve as the basis for a checklist for analyzing professional development needs.

In the complex enterprises that modern colleges and universities have become, the responsibility for leadership resided not only with the president, but with the other administrators in an executive team.

[1.] Although "management" is the term used in business, industry, and government, higher education prefers to use "administration." Both terms will be used interchangeably in this discussion.

Responsibility for visions, goals, and action

Development of vision. A higher education leader should
establish a vision for his or her institution that includes the
past, the present, and the future (Main 1987; Kerr 1984; Levinson 1968; Andrews 1966). This vision must relate to the larger
aims and values of the culture and society that lie beyond
higher education (Fisher 1978; Levinson 1968). A leader must
define a mission, provide a sense of direction, and designate
organizational priorities that, together, will serve as the unify-
ing purpose for the institution (Gardner 1986; Barnard 1968).

Development of goals, planning, and strategy. A leader must
draw others into that vision by making it tangible to constituencies both inside and outside the institution. A leader must
integrate facts, concepts, and stories into a coherent and mean-
ingful whole to make the vision compelling enough for others
to follow.

To turn a vision into a reality, a leader must utilize "techniques of leadership" (Millet 1976, p. 10), including creating
a frame of reference, setting priorities, describing a direction,
delineating outcomes, and establishing plans, strategies, programs, schedules, and procedures (Gardner 1986; Bennis 1984;
Kauffman 1982; Blake et al. 1981). A leader must then ensure
that these plans and strategies are efficiently and effectively im-
plemented within the value framework of the institution and society (Gardner 1986; Blyn and Zoerner 1982; Dressel 1981;
Keller 1983; Campanella et al. 1981; Scott 1978b; Cunningham et al. 1977; Richman and Farmer 1974; Henderson 1970;
Barnard 1968).

Development of innovation. Executives have a special
responsibility to innovate, initiate, and create by promoting
change. They must create organizations that are capable of constantly transforming themselves to meet the future needs of society and that can sustain innovation and creativity over time
(Main 1987; Kerr 1984; Whetten 1984; Birnbaum 1983; Keller
1983; Dressel 1981; Mortimer and McConnell 1978; Scott
1978b; Cunningham et al. 1977; Richman and Farmer 1974).

Development of consensus. Higher education is enriched by
the presence of many constituencies, each with individual priorities, demands, and agendas. Higher education leaders must
balance, on one hand, the necessity for loyalty to a common

venture with, on the other hand, the preservation and enhancement of diversity. In order to achieve a consensus, these administrators must reconcile competing purposes and mediate conflicting claims while establishing, through example and trust, that disagreement is acceptable (Gardner 1986; Kerr 1984; Whetten 1984; Scott 1978b; Mortimer and McConnell 1978; Mayhew 1974; Richman and Farmer 1974; Dodds 1962).

Development of decisions. In any organization, the responsibility for making the tough decisions resides with its executives. Chester Barnard, who established a framework for subsequent scholarship on leadership and management, felt that the entire "executive function centers around the process of decision making" (Ewing 1964, p. 14). But it is not enough just to make decisions. A leader must make wise decisions based on the reality of the present while laying the groundwork for the realization of the vision of the future (Whetten 1984; Birnbaum 1983; Keller 1983; Dressel 1981; Argyris and Cyert 1980; Eble 1978; Henderson 1970).

Development of resources. Without resources, the visions and goals cannot become reality. Thus, resource acquisition, optimization, allocation, and distribution are key to the success of all leadership and administrative responsibilities. Administrators must allocate resources to permit the greatest movement toward the goals and priorities of the institution as established through the planning process (Kerr 1984; Whetten 1984; Keller 1983; Campanella et al. 1981; Rausch 1980; Scott 1978b; Mayhew 1974; Levinson 1968).

Responsibility for operations
Administrators are responsible for all aspects of the complex enterprise that the modern college and university has become, including all of the institution's operations as well as the processes that make those operations work and interrelate. While it is generally regarded as a function of support services, from student affairs to the physical plant, it is more than just assuring their smooth running. This responsibility includes the design of the business, the securing of personnel, and the enforcement of values, standards, rules, and policies (Mortimer and McConnell 1978; Levinson 1968).

This category of responsibilities requires the most direct use of Millet's techniques of leadership. They include coordinating, planning, directing, managing, controlling, administering, monitoring, supervising, budgeting, reporting, staffing, organizing, supporting, maintaining, integrating, measuring, motivating, guiding, appraising, and executing (Gardner 1986; Birnbaum 1983; Kauffman 1982; Blake et al. 1981; Campanella et al. 1981; Dressel 1981; Rausch 1980; Scott 1978b; Richman and Farmer 1974; Livingston 1971).

Responsibility for relationships with the environment

This category of responsibility is bidirectional: from the environment to the institution and from the institution to the environment. Although all members of the academic community—administrators, faculty, and students—reach into the environment in their own ways and for their own purposes, only senior administrators can see the entire institutional enterprise and relate all of its activities to all aspects of the environment. The two-directional facet of this responsibility requires that officers participate extensively in activities outside the academic community (Kerr 1984; Millet 1976; Livingston 1971; Andrews 1966; Barnard 1968; Levinson 1968).

To meet this responsibility, administrators must search for developments in the outside world that will have an impact on the institution's present operations and on its goals for the future (Richman and Farmer 1974), which requires an awareness of trends and innovations beyond a single discipline, institution, or even the academy (Gaff et al. 1978). Leaders must evaluate and synthesize signals from the environment and use them to expand and strengthen the institution (Levinson 1968; Andrews 1966).

In the other direction, senior administrators have the responsibility of interpreting, for the public, their institution in specific and higher education in general. They must represent the institution for its tangible and practical benefits to individuals and for its symbolic value to society and culture. They must be both translators and spokespersons (Gardner 1986; Bennis 1984; Kerr 1984; Kauffman 1982; Blake et al. 1981; Dressel 1981).

Responsibility for people

Development of people. "People are the most abundant and most important resource of colleges and universities" (Green 1987, p. 1). Higher education institutions would have no purpose without faculty and students. Thus, finding and developing people is "one of the most important tasks of a manager, if not *the most* important" (Rausch 1980, p. 114). In higher education, this responsibility is heightened by society's expectation that colleges and universities will develop and test the leaders of tomorrow, the students, through education and its faculty through scholarship (Kerr 1984; Keller 1983; Blake et al. 1981; Campanella et al. 1981; Dressel 1981; Scott 1978b; Cunningham et al. 1977; Millet 1976; Richman and Farmer 1974; Drucker 1973; Levinson 1968; Dodds 1962).

Development of a working environment. In older books about leadership, this responsibility was described as the development of morale. More recent authors use the term "working environment," or "providing an environment and structure that adequately satisfies important human needs" (Richman and Farmer 1974, p. 21). In a good working environment, people will work better, create better, teach better, and learn better. An environment that encourages new ideas, risk taking, and creativity begins with senior administrators and permeates the institution for interpretation by middle-level administrators and faculty (Kerr 1984; Whetten 1984; Birnbaum 1983; Scott 1978b; Cunningham et al. 1977; Richman and Farmer 1974).

Development of communications. Without communications, none of the work of the institution is possible. The executive team must provide a basic system of communications that goes beyond telephone and computer networking systems to include policies of open discussion and an acceptance of all ideas. Administrators, particularly at the senior level, must personally keep everyone aware of the mission, goals, and values of the institution (Gardner 1986; Bennis 1984; Kauffman 1982; Barnard 1968).

Necessary Skills and Knowledge
Using Millet's concept of "techniques of leadership," the next step is to extrapolate from this list the skills and knowledge competencies most necessary for effective leadership and management. As academics have argued for centuries, to create a vision appropriate for a higher education institution, an executive needs a firm grounding in the purpose of the enterprise and the ways and means of its operations, which can come only from experience in the academy and a strong background in the

liberal arts (Kerr 1984; Scott 1978b; Fisher 1978, 1977; Bolman 1964).

Beyond these two basic criteria, executives also need to know much about the techniques of leadership, including a knowledge of the theory and behavior of organizations and people. Since their work involves turning a vision into a reality, they need to know about planning, strategy, and governance. They must know about management principles and operations so they can build smoothly functioning and efficient systems. They must know about evaluation and analysis so they can make better decisions. In order to relate their institutions to the environment, they must know about marketing. As leaders who are trying to develop consensus, they must know about politics and negotiations, and about relations with government, the media, and the public.

To develop resources, they need to know about financial management and control, resource allocation, and institutional advancement. For effective communications, they must know something about management information systems as well as have excellent written and oral communication skills (Gardner 1986; Dressel 1981; Argyris and Cyert 1980; Rausch 1980; Lusterman 1977; Fisher 1977; Millet 1976; Mayhew 1974; Henderson 1970; Bolman 1964; Enarson 1962). Most important, executives need to be able to integrate all of these skills, knowledge, and techniques to create and then fulfill their visions (Lusterman 1977).

There is a strong mythology in higher education that administrators of colleges and universities do not need to know about these techniques of leadership to do their job (Green *Forthcoming*; McDade 1986; Keller 1983; Moore et al. 1983). Many administrators argue that their job is to represent the institution and to ensure the best possible faculty, curriculum, and students. They argue that they have staff responsible for managing the business (Kanter and Wheatley 1978). But to ask the right questions of that staff and to know if the answers received are not just technically correct but truly right for the situation, a leader must understand the operations and processes involved (Kauffman 1982; Rausch 1980).

To organize that staff for optimum support, a leader must know something about organizations and the resources, both financial and human, that make the organizations work. The executives of the multimillion dollar enterprise that most colleges and universities have now become should know these things.

They should have a well-developed repertoire of management skills and leadership techniques to remain long as the leaders of those institutions and to ensure endurance of their institutions.

Several authors have tried to categorize the skills necessary for a successful executive. Digman (1980) defined three areas: technical skills (methods, processes, procedures, and techniques of analysis and management), human skills (the ability to build a team and to work effectively as a group member), and conceptual skills (the ability to see the whole, its parts, and their relationships). From his research on administrative development, Hodgkinson (1981) identified clear and definable managerial problem-solving skills as a necessary category. Although it is believed that "people skills" constituted the other important development area, he felt unclear about exactly what these skills were.

In his review of the leadership needs for the eighties, Argyris identified four skill area groups for administrators of colleges and universities: peer skills (the ability to establish and maintain networks), leadership skills (authority, power, and dependence), conflict-resolution skills (mediation, handling disturbances, and working under pressure), and information processing skills (collection, evaluation, organization, and dissemination of information) (Argyris and Cyert 1980).

Several studies have attempted to rank those leadership techniques of greatest importance and thus of greatest need to administrators. In four recent studies senior administrators were asked to identify and rank the skills and knowledge areas of particular importance to them. Digman (1980) surveyed 746 executive managers of 18 well-managed companies. Lutz and Ferrante (1972) reported a study by Parnell H. Hoffman of executives (principals and superintendents) of 35 school systems. McDonough-Rogers et al. (1982a, 1982b) surveyed 500 senior- and middle-level executives of the New York State government and the State University of New York (SUNY) system. McDade's unpublished study from 1985 included 170 senior administrators of colleges and universities (see table 1).

In all four studies, administrators ranked organizing and planning skills among the most important. These skills ranked first in the fields of secondary education and government, second in business, and fourth in higher education. Human relations skills such as team building, evaluating and appraising employees, motivating others, negotiating, and handling politics also ranked among the top five competencies for each

TABLE 1

MOST FREQUENT DEVELOPMENT NEEDS

Business (Digman 1980)	Secondary Education (Lutz & Ferrante 1972)	Government (McDonough-Rogers et al. 1982a, b)	Higher Education (McDade *Unpublished*)
1. Managing time	1. Long-range planning	1. Planning	1. Speaking publicly
1. Team building	2. Financial management/control	2. Program development, design	2. Delegating
2. Organizing, planning	3. Curriculum	3. Administration	3. Working with boards
2. Evaluating, appraising employees	4. Negotiations	4. Motivating subordinates	4. Planning
3. Coping with stress	5. Staffing	5. Interpersonal skills	4. Acquiring resources
3. Understanding human behavior	6. Student activism	6. Financial management/control	5. Working with governments
4. Self-analysis	7. Administration	7. Cost/benefit analysis	6. Budgeting time
4. Motivating others	8. Sensitivity training	8. Delegation of authority	7. Financial management/control
5. Budgeting	9. Urban youth	9. Leadership	8. Developing support
6. Setting objectives and priorities	10. Integration	9. Communication skills	9. Analyzing data
6. Holding effective meetings	11. Organizations	10. Delivery of goods, services	9. Conducting meetings
7. Oral communication	12. Intergovernment relationships	11. Legislative committee work	10. Cultivating constituency support
8. Labor/management relations	13. Business theory	12. Training and development techniques	11. Negotiating, resolving conflict
9. Decision making	14. State/national programs	13. State financial process	12. Motivating personnel
9. Developing strategies, policies		14. Media presentation	13. Framing programs, policies
10. Management control			14. Measuring, evaluating programs
10. Presentation skills			15. Establishing marketing strategy

NOTE: Duplicate numbers indicate a tie.

group. Financial management and control ranked second in importance for the secondary education administrators, fifth for the business and government executives, and seventh for the higher education leaders. Of note, the McDonough-Rogers study included administrators from the State University of New York system. Analysis showed great similarities between the skills of government executives and those of higher education.

The only significant difference was that the SUNY administrators were more involved in financial management (specifically, budgeting) and spent more time in meetings than did their government counterparts.

In McDade's study, higher education administrators were also asked to report their interest in attending professional development programs to increase specific leadership skills. Presidents wanted to learn more about planning models, administration, curriculum, issues of the future, and technology (in decreasing order of importance). Vice presidents of academic affairs wanted programs in curriculum, technology, faculty-related issues, planning models, and administration, while deans of the arts and sciences division sought development on faculty issues, followed by programs on topics relating to the future of higher education, issues relating to students, human relations, and the nature of organizations. Vice presidents of administration sought development opportunities in administration, future issues, finance and control, and planning models.

Top administrators of colleges and universities, like their counterparts in business, secondary education, and government, spend a great deal of time turning their visions into a future reality through planning. To this end, they know they need to further develop their planning skills and their understanding of the crucial issues of the future. Higher education leaders concentrate their energies and time on their constituencies, including boards of trustees, governments, faculty, students, and people in general, and, thus, wish to improve their skills in negotiations, meetings, and politics, and their knowledge of human relations, including motivation and interpersonal skills.

Emphasizing that the cornerstone of a college is its curriculum, administrators wish for additional insights into program design, development, and evaluation. Since they spend a great deal of time and effort in the acquisition, management, and control of resources, they wish to further understand these areas so they can initiate better policies and strategies.

Summary
Although the skills and knowledge necessary for administration vary depending upon level and function, there are a number of responsibilities common to all administration that dictate basic skills and knowledge. Those responsibilities can serve as a basis for analyzing the skills and knowledge needed for a par-

ticular job and for growth into other jobs. The checklist
provided in this chapter can serve as a basis for analyzing
strengths and weaknesses and for selecting professional development opportunities.

LESSONS FROM OTHER FIELDS

Management development is a major effort in most businesses, government organizations, and the military. With the exception of the field of education, organizations that do not focus on improving their management are dwarfed by those that are making major human resource investments in education and training. In most organizations, management development is an episodic, ongoing, formal process that is an integral part of the organizational system, culture, and corporate philosophy. In many organizations, it is simply expected that at every rung of the promotion ladder a manager will participate in a variety of development programs emphasizing both management skills and leadership techniques. Since most of the documentation on executive education is from the business world, the majority of this discussion will focus on corporate activities. Examples from government, service organizations, and the military will be included where appropriate.

Organizations that do not focus on improving their management are dwarfed by those that are making major human resource investments in education and training.

Overview of Management and Executive Development Activity

U.S. corporations annually spend nearly $60 billion on education programs for approximately 8 million students. This is roughly equivalent to the enrollment and yearly expenditures of the nation's 3,500 colleges and universities and about 1.5 percent of the GNP (Short 1987; Ingols 1986; Sonnenfeld and Ingols 1986; Eurich 1985; Fiske 1985; Sonnenfeld 1983). Although it is difficult to tabulate the exact amount, "industry sources estimate that 'much' of this money is spent on training for managers or other white-collar workers" (Ingols 1986, p. i).

Compared with five years ago, "a larger proportion of employees in all major job categories are now involved each year in formal training. . . . Growth rates of participation have been highest for managers" (Lusterman 1986, p. v). A 1983 report by Executive Development Associates on education in Fortune 500 companies concluded that "senior executives will almost double their hours of management education . . . as a demand for greater productivity . . . leads to an increased emphasis on management training at all levels" (Bolt 1987, p. 27).

Management education, as well as corporate education, is unevenly distributed. As would be expected, large, Fortune 500 corporations have developed more extensive executive education programming. In a survey of Fortune 500 corporations, Fresina found that 69 percent of responding companies (from a sample of 300) have executive education and, generally, they were the larger firms (1986). Smaller companies usually rely more on outside consultants, part-time training programs, and cooperative relationships with local educational institutions such as community colleges (Fresina 1986; Ingols 1986; Eurich 1985).

Industries with the highest investment in research and development have the most advanced education programs. It is no surprise that companies such as IBM, AT&T, Texas Instruments, Digital Equipment Corporation, ControlData, and Wang make the largest education expenditures (Eurich 1985).

The curricula of management education are most similar across different types of companies. Course sequencing is the clearest. "It is usually scheduled at regular transition points in individual career development. Training progresses in linear fashion from the first supervisory assignment to first-line manager, middle management, and on to corporate-level executives. . . . No other curricular area is laid out in so orderly and logical a sequence" (Eurich 1985, p. 63; Tichy 1987; Lusterman 1986; Main 1982; Atwell and Green 1981). In the military there are mandatory times in career progression when an officer returns to school (Ulmer 1987). In general, curriculum addresses four broad management areas: managing time, people, production and operations, and money.

There are important differences in the programs for top executives compared with those for beginning and middle managers. Senior-level programs address broader concerns such as "outside environmental factors, public policy issues, governmental relations and international politics, ethics and corporate social responsibility" (Eurich 1985, p. 66). More outside experts enter their classrooms, and they attend university programs or special institutes. These programs are frequently longer in length than other company programs. "As executives climb the career ladder, it's increasingly true that the information and knowledge they want are likely to be found not so much in libraries and data bases as in the minds of trusted colleagues" (Farson 1987, p. 44).

Although most programs contain an evaluation component, few include analysis, follow-up, pre- and post-testing, or cost accountability (Sonnenfeld and Ingols 1986). As in higher education, assessment of executive education and, thus, its objective worth is a hotly debated topic (Main 1982). Many corporations are quite open about their lack of rigorous evaluation but feel that the benefits of executive education are so obvious that the investment is worthwhile (Lusterman 1986; Schrader 1985). "Management development programs—and others with complex aims and distant payoffs—present the more formidable evaluation difficulties" (Lusterman 1986, p. 13).

Goals for Executive Education
At the bottom line, the goal of corporate education is to improve an organization's performance and, thus, its profits. Although it is difficult to establish direct links between all forms of corporate education and the bottom line, the link is strongly enough perceived that it is taken as an article of faith by organizations that provide professional development activities (Bolt 1987). It is no surprise, therefore, that fewer training departments were eliminated in recent recessions than had been in the recessions of the past decade (Lusterman 1986).

In addition to this preeminent objective of improving an organization's bottom line, business, government, and the military share other goals for executive development activities. Fresina and associates identified six current goals for executive education across all industries: individual development, succession planning, organizational development/change, strategy related, process/communicate information, and culture building (1986; Lusterman 1986; Schrader 1985). The U.S. Army has a set of doctrines that define leadership and serve as goals for its leadership-training courses (Ulmer 1987). Other common purposes include:

Recruitment and employee benefits. Most organizations try to provide competitive health care, retirement, and savings plans. If basic benefits are similar, companies need to provide "extras" to achieve an edge in recruiting and retaining outstanding employees. Education benefits, including training programs, tuition reimbursement, and opportunities for advanced degree work, are important determinants in the quality of work life (Eurich 1985; London 1985).

Orientation. Virtually every organization sponsors an orientation program for new employees. Successful organizations also offer programs for new managers with each promotion to explain expectations, roles, and corporate culture, and to introduce appropriate management skills and behaviors. Networks are expanded, communication is improved, and cooperation is increased as newly promoted managers see themselves as part of a larger entity (Sonnenfeld and Ingols 1986; Eurich 1985; London 1985).

Compensatory education and lifelong learning. Professional development includes updating the skills and knowledge of every employee, including managers. A Stanford spokesman explained, "Even an MBA who graduates from here knows it [the degree] will be obsolete in three or four years," while a Wang spokesman noted "professionals are probably going to have to go to school throughout their career . . . to stay abreast of their field. You'd better be prepared to continue your education for perhaps 40 years" (Short 1987, p. 25). Corporate education is quite concerned with technological advancements and organizational and management theory. " 'Technological change,' a Xerox executive says, 'is the main force now driving education and training in our company. One of our major challenges is keeping our people at the leading edge' " (Lusterman 1986, p. 1; Short 1987; Schwartz 1987; Eurich 1985).

Specificity to corporate strategies. More and more organizations are tying executive education to their strategies. Increasingly, employees are viewed as assets worthy of improvement. Corporate strategy and business objectives become the focus of education programs as managers move up the ladder (Short 1987; Bolt 1987; Lusterman 1986; Sonnenfeld and Ingols 1986; Eurich 1985).

Preparation for a world marketplace. In the face of global competition, employees at every level need to understand the expanded world in which they now function. To this end, AT&T periodically runs corporate policy seminars for its top managers "to increase understanding of critical outside forces" (London 1985, p. 191; Bolt 1987; Sonnenfeld and Ingols 1986; Eurich 1985; Main 1982).

Preparation for future roles and responsibilities. Many organizations have long recognized that future leadership will come from their own ranks. Promotion from within requires investment in identifying and training leaders. "Writing 25 years ago, Jay W. Forrester of the Sloan School of Management at MIT argued that 'some 25 percent of the total working time of all persons in the corporations should be devoted to preparation for their future roles' " (Eurich 1985, p. 47). Large firms often offer a continuum of programs for job entry and follow-up programs at each level of management. For example, GE managers participate in development programs at each stage of their careers (Tichy 1987; Bolt 1987; Lusterman 1986;

Sonnenfeld and Ingols 1986; Schrader 1985; Sonnenfeld 1983; Digman 1980).

Sources and Types of Professional
Development for Executives
Business, industry, government, and the military depend on a diversity of program types to serve different professional development needs. Certain types of sponsors have specialized in particular categories of programs, although there is considerable overlap. Increasingly, large organizations are developing in-house human resource staffs to produce a total programming system for employees.

In-house executive educational programs
Most commonly, executive education takes place in programs, seminars, workshops, and institutes offered at the workplace. While we hear about the largest corporations and their facilities, it is estimated that a building or entire campus devoted to education exists on more than 400 business sites. Although the titles may vary—college, university, institute, education center—the activities inside are similar (Watkins 1983). The strength of in-house programs lies in their ability to explain "how we do it here at our company" (Schrader 1985).

The Xerox Center in Leesburg, Virginia, is probably the largest of these centers. A faculty of 250 work with over 1,000 students at a time in programs ranging from technical courses to advanced management and leadership seminars (Scott 1978b).

General Electric has had a corporate education center since 1956, now located at Crotonville, New York, with a mission "to make GE managers more action oriented, more risk oriented, more people oriented. It's supposed to develop leaders, not just managers" (Dobrzynski 1987). Its main program, the 13-week Advanced Management Course, focuses on company philosophy and general management. In 1983, GE spent approximately $100 million on training and development with "10 percent of that amount spent on management development alone. Estimates of participation in GE corporate management education for 1980 suggest that 5,000 executives were involved in centralized internal programs in the United States; 25,000 managers participated in decentralized programs offered domestically; and another 3,000 were involved in programs outside the United States'' (Sonnenfeld 1983, p. 291; Tichy 1987; Lusterman 1986).

Other outstanding examples include the RCA campus (New Jersey), Holiday Inn University (Mississippi), McDonald's Hamburger University (Chicago), Sun Institute's Learning Center (Pennsylvania), ARCO's campus for top executives (Santa Barbara), New England Telephone's Learning Center (Massachusetts), and Western Electric's Corporate Education Center (New Jersey) (Eurich 1985; Sonnenfeld 1983).

The Army, Navy, Coast Guard, and Air Force maintain their own executive institutes such as the Naval War College in Newport, Rhode Island. Each service has in-house groups, such as the Center for Army Leadership, to develop materials, programs, and assessment procedures (Ulmer 1987). Similar programs are offered to government civil servants at the Federal Executive Institute in Charlottesville, Virginia.

Fortune 500 companies—IBM, AT&T, Procter and Gamble, Raytheon, and Johnson and Johnson—offer advanced management and leadership courses. Many of them are of such high quality that they have come to command a respect equal to the certification of academic degrees (Sonnenfeld 1983).

University-based executive development programs
Among the oldest continuing professional development programs for business executives are those available from leading university business schools. These programs trace their roots to the year-long Sloan Fellows Program of the Massachusetts Institute of Technology, established in 1931, and Harvard's 13-week Advanced Management Program (AMP), established in 1943 (Billy 1987, p. v; Sonnenfeld and Ingols 1986; Main 1982). University-based programs expose executives to viewpoints different from their own and their companies through interaction with faculty and classmates with diverse experiences (Schrader 1985).

The 1987 edition of *Bricker's International Directory of University Executive Programs* lists 78 U.S. general management programs, six on the business environment, 23 on leadership and organizations, six on the management of technology, and nine on government, education, and health organizations, in addition to 81 functional management programs. In 1987 more than 14,000 executives attended university residential general and functional management programs at more than 50 universities in the United States and Canada (''Bricker Bulletin'' 1987a, p. 4). Several thousand more participated at 20 institutions in Europe, the United Kingdom, Ireland, and Australia.

Out of a total of 59 schools (196 programs), Harvard enrolled 11.8 percent (1,422) of all participants (12,011) for 26.2 percent (8,837) of all participant-weeks (33,700), the difference being accounted for by the length of the Harvard programs. The top ten schools accounted for 68.4 percent of participants and 64 percent of participant-weeks ("Bricker Bulletin" 1987b, p. 3).

Ivy League schools offer the largest number of programs (Harvard University, 17; Columbia University, 12; Massachusetts Institute of Technology, 9; Northwestern University, 11; University of Pennsylvania, 17; Stanford University, 13). State flagship campuses also offer large numbers of programs (University of Michigan, 8; Pennsylvania State University, 13; and University of Virginia, 11) (Billy 1987).

Formats vary. They range in length from a week to nine months, with three to four weeks as the mode. Although most programs are one residential session, many involve several sessions of days or weeks.

Colleges and universities also offer programs for the professional development of government executives, for example, the Harvard University Program for Senior Executives in State and Local Government and the Program for Senior Managers in Government.

In addition to the previously described programs that focus on management and leadership skills, a number of university-based programs specialize in intellectual renewal.

Another approach is offered by the Aspen Institute and by programs such as the Stanford University Executive Program in the Humanities. Their purpose is to provide intellectual refreshment and an opportunity to view the world more broadly and deeply than is possible in the pressure cooker of daily work (Gardner 1987, p. 23).

Institutions offering humanities-based professional development programs include Dartmouth College, Indiana University, Wabash College, Washington and Lee University, and Williams College (Billy 1987).

A third group of university-based programs are collaborative efforts of colleges and corporations. They include programs tailored to the training needs of a specific company. Most often, collaboration is with a community college, although some exist with four-year institutions. These programs are usually more flexible in format, location, and facilities. They often include a blend of campus learning and on-the-job applications (Lusterman 1986; Nash and Hawthorne 1987; Sonnenfeld and Ingols 1986).

Commercial vendors

Management programs are offered by associations such as the NTL Institute and the American Management Association (AMA), the country's largest training organization. Typical programs from the more than 5,000 one- to three-day courses offered each year by AMA include "First-Line Management," "Leadership Skills for Executives," "A Manager's Guide to Financial Analysis," and "How to Manage Administrative Operations" (AMA 1987; Main 1982). AMA also offers a special four-course series for managers of service organizations. The advantage of participation in these programs is the opportunity to meet managers from a wide spectrum of organizations and functions.

Commercial vendors such as Xerox Learning Systems, Wilson Learning, and Forum Corporation, also prepare and package programs to meet specific needs and goals of a company or industry. These vendors can be extremely flexible in their programming and can create new programs within a short time frame to address new issues. Unlike in-house programs, which often recycle the same ideas, consultants and commercial vendors can provide an infusion of new blood, new thoughts, and new techniques (Main 1982). On the other hand, quality may vary considerably across programs (Sonnenfeld and Ingols 1986). For some activities, the use of commercial vendors is a more cost-effective alternative to internal staffing and can provide specialized expertise not available in the organization (Lusterman 1986).

Corporate colleges

Some organizations have found that their products and activities have become so specialized that colleges and universities no longer provide supporting academic work or degrees. To fill this gap, several have developed their own degree programs

(Nash and Hawthorne 1987; Short 1987). While the majority of these degree-granting institutions are in engineering and computers, an increasing number are in business administration.

It is difficult to count these programs because they are so unique. Eurich identified 18 corporate educational institutions, which she described as "an odd assortment of types and hybrids that challenge clear definition" (1985, p. 87; Fiske 1985). Of these 18, seven offer management degrees, for example, the M.S. in Financial Services Management from the American College (Bryn Mawr, Pa.), sponsored by the National Association of Life Underwriters, and the M.S. in Administration and M.S. in Management from the Arthur D. Little Management Institute (Cambridge, Mass.), sponsored by Arthur D. Little, Inc. Eurich estimated that by 1988, eight more corporations would create 20 additional college-level degree programs (1985, p. xi). A similar study by Nash and Hawthorne concluded that "at present, 21 corporate colleges in 11 states have degree-granting authority" (1987, p. 20). Of these 21, three offer management degrees, one offers a policy degree, six offer manufacturing degrees, and two feature technical degrees (1987, pp. 16–19). One entity, the Wang Institute of Graduate Studies, merged with Boston University in 1987. All indications point to an expanding corporate education sector at all levels.

International programs

Professional development for executives is not restricted to the U.S. European organizations such as the International Management Development Institute (IMEDE) in Lausanne, Switzerland, the International Management Institute (IMI) in Geneva, Switzerland, and the European Institute of Business Administration (INSEAD) in Fontainebleau, France, offer a full range of professional development programs, including specific courses for executives. The majority of these programs are taught in English. Other European schools with significant reputations conduct classes in other languages ("Bricker Bulletin" 1986).

Nine universities and the Niagara Institute offer programs in Canada. Similar programs are offered throughout Australia, southeast Asia, and India both by local universities and by American universities. For example, the University of Virginia offers a management program in Australia, while Harvard University operates a program, "Multinational Marketing Management," in Europe (Billy 1987). Some of the Soviet satellite countries have started advanced management programs. In 1970 two major advanced management programs for industrial executives were launched in the Soviet Union (Drucker 1973).

Lessons from the Most Successful Programs

Important lessons can be learned by studying the most successful management and executive programs of business, government, and the military. Higher education institutions considering an investment in the management and leadership development of their administrators would be wise to investigate these programs.

Senior management's active role

A common comment in profiles of successful programs is the importance of the involvement and commitment of the senior executive team and, in particular, the CEO. "The CEO is central. Without the understanding and commitment at this level, leadership development is impossible" (Tichy 1987, p. 41; Bolt 1985). This commitment includes direct involvement of all senior executives in the planning of training, the participation by senior executives as teachers and students in development activities, and by serving as role models in the pursuit of education (Bolt 1987; Golde 1987; Greiner 1987; Short 1987; Lusterman 1986).

Training's position in the hierarchy is an important indicator of senior management's active role in education.

> *A most important factor determining the extent and success of an industry's program is the position of the person responsible for it. The higher the officer in charge of education, the more it reflects the commitment of the corporation to the program. To succeed, the chief executive officer has to want it. And the appointment of a corporate level executive for education will have the greatest impact on managers down the line, who permit the employee time off for study* (Eurich 1985, p. 51).

Although top executives may talk about the importance of professional development, lower-level supervisors actually make the decisions and allocate the funds from their budgets. Employees are quick to realize that what senior executives do is usually more important than what they say. Top executives need to develop management and leadership skills as much as other employees do (Golde 1987).

Clarity of the educational mission
Those organizations reaping the most rewards from education explicitly state its importance as the key investment in their employees (Bolt 1987; Lusterman 1986; Eurich 1985). This strategy usually appears in widely disseminated educational statements that "specify the firm's stand on such dimensions as (1) targeted populations, (2) relative emphasis on job/task-skill improvement versus longer-run career enhancement, (3) links to other career system variables (e.g., hiring, assignments, exiting), and (4) links to other organizational change efforts" (Sonnenfeld 1983, p. 307; Lusterman 1986; Bolt 1985).

The rewards of education are not coincidental because the investment and emphasis have been carefully planned, executed, and integrated into the life of these organizations. As senior executives learn what education can contribute to the organization, they demand education for all levels of employees as an integral part of the organization's culture (Bolt 1987).

Need for development activities to be coordinated, integrated, and purposeful
The management development programs with the most impact are not one shot or random. As part of the organization's succession planning, programming is periodic, coordinated with promotions, job challenges, and opportunities, and carefully integrated into jobs. Educational objectives are explicit, both for the organization as a whole and for individuals. Stages of development activities are linked for continuity. Programs produce definable skills with direct application to the job with a needs-driven orientation (Bolt 1987; Golde 1987; Greiner 1987; Tichy 1987; Lusterman 1986).

Organizations deriving the most benefit from professional development have so thoroughly assimilated training activities into the mainstream that the programs closely support the participants' jobs and their jobs provide planned opportunities "to use the knowledge, skills, and attitudes learned in training" (Clement 1981, p. 11).

Summary
Management development is a major effort in most businesses, the government, and the military. These organizations have

found it to be a good investment in terms of the bottom line as well as in more intangible ways such as individual development, succession planning, organizational development and change, and culture building. Professional development is provided by in-house educational programs, university-based programs, commercial vendors, corporate colleges, and international programs. Organizations that have reaped significant benefits from executive education share common characteristics: senior management is significantly and visibly committed and involved, the educational mission of the organization is clear, and development activities are coordinated and closely integrated into the mainstream of operations.

A SURVEY OF PROGRAMS

A variety of programs exists to meet the professional development needs of administrators. These programs vary by mission, educational goals, content, intended audience, format, pedagogy, length, site, size, and sponsor. Every issue of the *Chronicle of Higher Education* lists professional development programs sponsored by well-known institutions and associations, open to a wide assortment of academic and nonacademic executives from the entire country. In addition, there is a wealth of other programs open by special invitation to members of the sponsoring organization or advertised on a regional basis through less formal channels. An administrator must look carefully to identify programs appropriate to his or her needs and level of expertise and background. (See table 2 for a display of representative programs by intended audience and position level.)

The professional development programs can be loosely organized into four types or models. Although this typology overlaps to some extent, it provides a useful mechanism for categorizing programs and comparing purposes, audiences, lengths, and costs. (See the appendix for the addresses of the major programs and sponsors listed in this section.) The following discussion includes only the major programs or representative types of programs and is not meant to be all-inclusive. For a more complete listing of available programs, consult the directories listed in the appendix.

An administrator must look carefully to identify programs appropriate to his or her needs and level of expertise and background.

National Institutes and Internships
These extended and intensive professional development programs are among the oldest and most prestigious in higher education. Although the number of national institutes is small, the total of their alumni in senior posts is large. In general, they have the following characteristics:

- Minimum of two weeks in length or meet regularly as a class over a year;
- Sponsored by prestigious universities and higher education associations;
- Held at the campus of the sponsoring institution or at a host institution for internships;
- Usually require institutional nomination or endorsement;
- Highly competitive application process;
- Participation is national or even international;

TABLE 2
REPRESENTATIVE PROGRAMS BY INTENDED AUDIENCE

	President	Senior	Lower Senior	Upper Middle	Middle	Entry
For Academic Administrators						
ACAD Workshops			X	X	X	
Academic Leadership Institute (AASCU)		X	X			
ACE Fellows				X	X	X
Chairing the Academic Department (ACE)				X	X	
Institute for the Management of Lifelong Education (MLE)	X	X	X	X	X	
Institute for Trustee Leadership (AGB)	X					
National Conference of Deans				X	X	
Presidents Seminars (ACE)	X					
Troutbeck Program	X					
For Academic and Nonacademic Administrators						
College Management Program		X	X	X	X	
HERS/Bryn Mawr			X	X	X	X
HERS/Wellesley			X	X	X	X
Institute for Educational Management (IEM)	X	X	X	X		
Management Development Program				X	X	X
For Nonacademic Administrators						
Business Management Institutes (SACUBO/EACUBO/WACUBO/CACUBO)		X	X	X		
Institute for Student Personnel (NASPA/ACE)			X	X	X	
Williamsburg Development Institute		X	X	X	X	X
Summer Institute on College Admissions				X	X	X

Key (representative titles for each category)
President: Chief executive officer of an institution or system
Senior: Provost, Vice President, system officer
Lower Senior: Associate, Assistant Vice President
Upper Middle: Dean; Special or Executive Assistant to
Middle: Assistant & Associate Dean, Director; Assistant to
Entry: Department Chair, Admissions/Financial Aid Officer

- Participation from all types of institutions and all types of institutional positions;
- Follow-up available through receptions at national conventions, seminars, and newsletters;
- Attendance at a specific national institute is only once in a lifetime, although an administrator may participate in different programs in this category at different career stages;
- Focus on broad higher education issues, management techniques and processes, and leadership development.

The ACE Fellows program and internships

The oldest of these programs is the ACE Fellows sponsored by the American Council on Education. The program is designed to identify and train future leaders for progressively responsible positions in higher education. Participants are generally faculty members or first-level academic administrators who have shown a strong ability for and interest in management (ACE 1987a; Stauffer 1975; Creager 1971a, 1971b, 1966). Typically, participants are in entry-, middle-, or upper middle–level positions such as department chair, director, assistant dean, and assistant to the president.

For many, an ACE Fellowship was the springboard to senior administrative positions. Of the 843 ACE Fellows over the past 20 years, 109 (13 percent) have become presidents and 378 others (44 percent) have served as vice presidents, associate or assistant vice presidents, and deans (ACE 1987b; Kroger 1984). Fellows spend an internship year on another campus, where they work with campus leaders, manage special projects, and observe senior officers in every phase of their jobs. A Fellow may choose to stay on his or her own campus, but ACE discourages this option because it diminishes the educational experience. Fellows who elect this option are required to spend at least some time on another campus.

Fellows also attend at least three major seminars on financial management, legal issues such as collective bargaining and affirmative action, and government issues, including meeting with members of Congress and executive branch officials (Bray 1987). In addition, they participate in activities at the annual ACE convention.

Classes average 42 Fellows. Although male participants greatly outnumbered women (10 percent between 1965 and 1970) during the early years of the program, since 1970 women have represented 35 percent of the participants. The number of

minority fellowships has risen from 7 percent during 1965 to 1970 to 25 percent since 1980 (ACE 1987b).

Each Fellow is linked with a Mentor, a specially selected senior officer who works with the Fellow, monitors his or her activities, and provides important advice and support. Benefits accrue not only to the Fellow, but also to the host campus where the Fellow trains and works for a year, and especially to the senior administrator Mentor who works with the Fellow. Daniel H. Perlman, president of Suffolk University, Boston, an ACE Fellow 1972–73 and a Mentor 1982–83 stated:

The ACE Program has served a critical role in preparing new leaders for American higher education. Having been both a Mentor and Fellow, I can personally attest to the quality and value of this unique program. My Fellowship year was instrumental in preparing me to assume a deanship and then a presidency. More recently, as a Mentor, the exchanges with my Fellow gave me a fresh perspective on my own institution (ACE 1987a, p. 1).

Other internships follow the ACE pattern. The California State University system offers an in-house internship program similar in format and organization to the ACE Fellows program. Interns are chosen from the system's 19 campuses for a year's experience working with a senior officer on another campus. As with the ACE Fellows, although the interns are generally from the faculty and mid-level administration, significant professional development benefit accrues to the senior administrator mentor as well as to the intern.

The role of mentor within the context of a well-organized fellowship program should not be overlooked as a substantial professional development experience for a senior-level administrator. Applying the adage that it is usually the teacher who learns the most, mentors learn by teaching their younger proteges, by looking at the world through their younger and perhaps less biased eyes, and by reformulating their thinking in response to questions from the intern. In terms of human development theory, this is known as the additive stage of professional development. During this career phase, senior executives, serving as mentors, transmit "their commitment to and knowledge of the field. In turn, they might replenish their own commitment and knowledge through lifelong learning" (Moore and Young 1987, p. 21). The advantage of these programs is that they provide a structured, organized framework for the mentor/fellow relationship with guidance for the learning experience.

The Institute for Educational Management

The second oldest program in this group is the Institute for Educational Management (IEM), co-sponsored by the Graduate Schools of Business Administration and Education of Harvard University. Founded in 1970, IEM has nearly 2,000 alumni from more than 500 colleges and universities. Participants live on the Harvard campus and attend classes six days a week for four weeks. The case study courses, in areas such as marketing, financial management, planning, labor relations, and higher education law, are designed to provide participants with a broad view of higher education administration with a focus on the unique policy-setting responsibilities of senior executives (IEM 1987b).

Participants describe the experience as "an intellectual boot camp," "incredibly challenging," and "far beyond my most ambitious expectations" (McDade 1984, p. 13). Charles C. Schroeder, vice president of student development, St. Louis University, and a member of the class of 1983, recounted that

> *For me, the greatest value was the chance to snap a few frames from the motion picture of my life and do something radically different. It's a significant renewal experience—the opportunity to step out of my traditional routine and to participate in a whole new array of experiences, relationships, . . . the chance to look at everything with a fresh perspective* (McDade 1986, p. 47).

Current classes range from 90 to 95 members. Most participants are presidents, vice presidents, or deans in both academic and nonacademic fields in institutions or hold senior positions in system offices, state boards of higher education, associations, and foundations. Participants must be sponsored by their institution. "IEM is the most senior and by far the most expensive—at more than $200 a day—of the management institutes. . . . The most prestigious among any of the institutes, it attracts a far higher proportion of presidents among its applicants than any of the others" (Green *Forthcoming*).

Part of the original mission of IEM was to provide access for women and minorities to senior administrative positions. Dur-

ing the past five years women have averaged 30 percent of
each class, while minorities have averaged 24 percent. For the
past five years, international participants have averaged 8.6
percent of each class, including representatives from Mexico,
Switzerland, Scotland, Denmark, Hong Kong, Australia, and
the Philippines (IEM 1987a).

The Management Development Program
In 1986 IEM launched the Management Development Program
(MDP), a two-week institute for middle-level academic and
nonacademic administrators. It is designed to broaden management perspectives and leadership skills while exploring the
unique role and mission of higher education in today's society.
Participants typically are in middle-level to first-tier senior positions, with the majority holding titles such as department
chair, director, assistant and associate dean, dean, assistant and
associate vice president. The classes of 85 participants have averaged 44 percent women and 27 percent minorities (MDP
1987a, 1987b).

The Institute for the Management of Lifelong Education
Co-sponsored by Harvard University and the College Board,
the Institute for the Management of Lifelong Education (MLE),
is for "administrators, planners, program heads, and faculty
concerned with the design or implementation of lifelong education" (MLE 1987, p. 2). Founded in 1979, this two-week
residential program is structured much like the Institute for
Educational Management and the Management Development
Program, using a faculty drawn from Harvard and other outstanding practitioners.

The College Management Program
Another national institute for both academic and nonacademic
administrators is the College Management Program (CMP),
launched in 1976. In this institute,

> *College and senior executives work with fellow executives
> and an experienced faculty to address such issues as stra-
> tegic planning, management, marketing, budgeting, financial
> analysis, situational leadership, decision making, and the
> personal computer as a management tool* (CMP 1987, p. 2).

The CMP capitalizes on the management and computer science

strengths of Carnegie-Mellon University. Thus the three-week program has a more technical and quantitative emphasis than the other national institutes. The program is administered by the office of Executive Education of Carnegie-Mellon's School of Urban and Public Affairs, which also runs programs for executives of other fields.

Carnegie-Mellon's president, Richard Cyert, and economist, Herbert Simon, are deeply involved with the program. Other faculty include higher education leaders such as George Keller, John D. Millet, and Neil S. Bucklew. The three-week curriculum focuses on strategic planning; budgeting; accounting and financial analysis; marketing; selecting, evaluating, and developing faculty; and the computer as a management tool. The average class size is 35, with 21 percent women (Green *Forthcoming*).

A participant commented that the program "exposed me to a wide range of issues that affect institutions of higher learning in the 1980s and did so in a way that allowed me time for reflection" (CMP 1987, p. 9).

HERS/Bryn Mawr and Wellesley
The Higher Education Resource Services (HERS) supports two national institutes specifically for women in both academic and nonacademic jobs. Since 1976 the Summer Institute for Women in Higher Education Administration, co-sponsored by HERS/Mid-America and Bryn Mawr College, has groomed women faculty and middle managers for senior management positions. The program

> is designed for professional women in higher education, both faculty and staff, who wish to prepare themselves for further administrative responsibilities [that] require both the effective and creative use of existing talent and the acquisition of new skills (Bryn Mawr College and HERS 1987, p. 1).

Participants in the HERS/Bryn Mawr program are typically faculty members or middle-level administrators (Green *Forthcoming*). In addition, the primary responsibility areas of members of the 1987 class included faculty (20 percent), administrative services (34 percent), business/finance (8 percent), academic affairs (16 percent), external affairs (8 percent), student services (12 percent), and library (2 percent) (Bryn Mawr and HERS, Mid-America 1987b).

The HERS/Bryn Mawr program typically includes international participants, with Canada, Sweden, Wales, Iran, Nigeria, and the Netherlands recently represented. Its core courses focus on academic governance, administrative uses of the computer, management and leadership, human relations skills, budgeting, and finance. Class size averages 75 participants (Bryn Mawr College and HERS 1987; Hornig 1978).

A program similar in content is offered by HERS/New England at Wellesley College. Participants attend a series of five seminars over a period of a year. Both programs are unique in that they devote significant attention to career development for participants by examining "institutional structures in general and one's own institutional setting in particular; tokenism; planning a career path; career mapping; resume analysis; development of networks and other support systems" (Wellesley College and HERS 1987, p. 3).

Programs for executives in business and industry
A very small but growing number of higher education administrators are enrolling in college and university programs designed for the professional development of executives from business and industry. The grandfather of the national institute model is the Advanced Management Program (AMP) offered by Harvard University's Business School. This 11-week program explores the specifics of financial management and control as well as the more general topics of long-range planning and leadership development. Approximately 1 percent of the AMP alumni who work at colleges and universities were presidents or chancellors of a system at the time of their participation. Other examples include the Executive Development Program of Cornell University, the Management Development Program and Advanced Management Development Program of Boston University, and the Executive Development Program and Advanced Executive Program of Northwestern University.

General notes on national institutes
Despite the variety of program types in the national institute category, courses are similar (see table 3). The general curricula of national institutes emphasize primarily the development of management knowledge and skills—through courses in finance, marketing, law, and organizational theory—and, secondarily, the exploration of higher education issues. Within the management area, participants gain a broad understanding of

principles and theories and, depending on the program, develop a variety of tangible skills ranging from how to use a computer to financial analysis techniques. Because national institutes are generally sponsored by prestigious institutions or associations, they are able to attract top flight professors and distinguished practitioners to join their faculties.

It is no surprise that national institutes and internships offer their alumni a strong national and, for some programs, international network of peers. After completion of the program, each offers an infrastructure of alumni workshops, newsletters, and receptions so that alumni can continue to develop their contacts. Alumni cite the acquisition of contacts and friendships as a major and often unexpected benefit. Intensive course schedules, the length of the programs, and the residential components create camaraderie that runs deep. The friendships made within a particular class expand as graduates join the program's alumni network. It is a statement of the strength and popularity of these programs that each has enthusiastic and loyal alumni. ACE Fellows meet every year at the ACE convention to renew friendships and trade stories (Heller 1984a). IEM sponsors well-attended receptions at major conventions and welcomes alumni back to Harvard for an annual reunion seminar.

Alumni cite the acquisition of contacts and friendships as a major and often unexpected benefit.

Administrative Conferences

Although similar in organization to the national institutes, administrative conferences differ in length, instructional focus, and range of participation. They have the following general characteristics:

- From several days to less than two weeks in length;
- Sponsored by institutions, associations, and foundations;
- Held at a variety of locations ranging from university campuses to resorts;
- Institutional endorsement and sponsorship usually not required;
- Usually acceptance on a first-come, first-served basis;
- Participation generally from a particular type of institution, a specific function area, or a certain level of administrators;
- Participation generally national but rarely international;
- Follow-up depends on program, but usually not very extensive;

TABLE 3
AN OVERVIEW OF MAJOR NATIONAL INSTITUTES

Title	Sponsor	Length	Timing	Founding
ACE Fellows	American Council on Education	Academic year	Academic year	1965
College Management Program (CMP)	Carnegie-Mellon University	21 days	Summer	1976
Institute for Educational Management (IEM)	Harvard University	28 days	Summer	1970
Institute for the Management of Lifelong Education (MLE)	Harvard University, College Board	12 days	Summer	1979
Management Development Program (MDP)	Harvard University	13 days	Summer	1986
Management Institute for Women in Higher Education (HERS/Wellesley)	HERS/New England, Wellesley College	Five three-day sessions	Over one year	1979
Summer Institute for Women in Higher Education Administration (HERS/Bryn Mawr)	HERS/Mid-America, Bryn Mawr College	26 days	Summer	1976

- An administrator may attend a program annually or on a regular, repeating basis;
- Focus on management tasks and leadership responsibilities in the context of an institutional type or functional area.

Like the national institutes, many of the administrative conferences are held on college or university campuses. Some

TABLE 3 (Continued)

Location	Size	Cost	Curriculum
Varies	42	$700 minimum + $2500 travel	Budgeting; Financial Management; Planning; Law; Collective Bargaining; Personnel Issues; Leadership; Curriculum; Federal Policy
Pittsburgh, PA	35	$3700	Strategic Planning; Budgeting, Accounting & Financial Analysis; Marketing; Selecting, Evaluating & Developing Faculty; Computer Management as a Tool
Cambridge, MA	95	$6300	Monitoring the Environment; Setting Directions; Marshaling Resources & Support; Managing Implementation
Cambridge, MA	80	$2420	Adult Learning & Development; Organizational Management (Marketing & Financial Management); Institutional Leadership & Change
Cambridge, MA	85	$3000	Leadership (Organizations, Issues, Small Groups) Management (Law, Decision Making, Financial Management, Human Resource Management, Faculty Policy & Administration); Higher Education (Cultural Diversity, Issues)
Wellesley, MA	50	$1350	Fiscal Management; Managing Organizations; Information Systems & Application; Strategic Planning; Professional Development
Bryn Mawr, PA	75–80	$3700	Academic Governance; Administrative Uses of Computers; Management and Leadership; Professional Development; Human Relations; Finance and Budgeting

administrative conferences are held in resort areas, and many provide substantial free time for recreational activities. The resort ambience seems to encourage more informal exchange among participants. Since a spouse can be a great asset to a college or university administrator, especially a senior officer, many of the recent programs have included spouses for all or part of the conference. These seminars are most often sponsored by national associations specifically for their members. Formats vary considerably from a version nearer that of a shortened national institute to a form more like that of an extended seminar.

National Conference of Academic Deans

The oldest administrative seminar for academic administrators is sponsored by Oklahoma State University. Also known as the Stillwater Conference for its location in Stillwater, Oklahoma, the program began in 1941 and has been held every year since 1948. The continuing goal is to examine "Qualities of Academic Leadership."

> *The conference functions through an invitation list and a nucleus of loyal participants who come back year after year. . . . The number of participating deans each year averages 70–75. These come from nearly all the states, coast to coast, and they represent all kinds of schools. . . . Participants are academic vice presidents, deans of colleges, liberal arts deans at universities, and also deans of education, graduate and other university schools. . . . The commonality that holds it all together is a deep concern with maintaining effectiveness in the deanship* (Karman 1983).

Recent themes of the four-day seminar have included "The Economics of Higher Education," "The Role of the Dean in the Search for Educational Excellence," and "Education for the Twenty-First Century: The Professoriate, Curricula, and Applied Technology" (Conference of Academic Deans 1987; Karman and Gardiner 1985).

Programs from ACE's Center for Leadership Development

The Center for Leadership Development and Academic Administration of the American Council on Education has sponsored many programs through the years for specific groups of administrators. One of its best known continuing programs is for presidents. Offered every year or every other year, this program offers new presidents an opportunity to "meet with veteran presidents and other higher education officials . . . for pragmatic advice, off-the-cuff tidbits, and nuts-and-bolts strategies" while providing opportunities for reflection and renewal for more seasoned presidents (Heller 1984b, p. 16; ACE 1987b).

This presidential colloquium focuses on a different theme each year. The 1986 seminar, "The Effective CEO" held at the Copper Mountain Resort in Colorado, addressed leadership issues such as working with a board, building a presidential team, and relating to the media through case studies in presidential leadership. The 1988 program focuses on "Moral Leadership in Higher Education." Other ACE programs, such as the 1985 program, "The 6,000-Minute Sabbatical," are more renewal oriented.

Another popular ACE program for academic administrators is "Chairing the Academic Department—For Deans, Division and Department Chairpersons." Sessions focus on the roles, powers, and responsibilities of the division leader; the department or division in the context of the institution; conflict and faculty morale; and faculty selection, evaluation, and development. John Zacharis, vice president of academic affairs and dean of the college, Emerson College, Boston, remembered:

> It . . . provided a broad range of data about colleges and universities so that I could see Emerson and my role in the broad picture. I saw that my problems were similar to others. It put me in contact with similar people. It was a relief to find out that my experiences were no different than people in similar positions at other schools. It gave me the confidence to deal at this level. It was a measuring against peers and I felt an equal (McDade 1986, p. 56).

Other programs for academic administrators

Other representative programs for academic administrators include the "Summer Seminar on Academic Administration" sponsored by Texas A&M University and the "New Deans Seminar" sponsored by the American Assembly of Collegiate Schools of Business (AACSB). The American Association of State Colleges and Universities (AASCU) offers a five-day seminar, "Academic Leadership Institute," for new academic vice presidents in conjunction with its annual summer conference. Within a special subcategory is the "Institute for Trustee Leadership" sponsored by the Association of Governing Boards (AGB) for board members (trustees) and chief executive officers. The American Conference of Academic Deans sponsors workshops for academic deans during the annual meeting of the

Association of American Colleges. In 1987 the American Association of State Colleges and Universities (AASCU) introduced a seminar for new academic vice presidents at its annual summer conference. AASCU sponsors a calendar of seminars throughout the year for presidents, vice presidents, and other academic officers of member state colleges and universities.

Programs for nonacademic administrators

Other programs exist for administrators interested in specific areas of institutional management. The range of programs in this category is too vast for detailed coverage here. Representative examples include the Williamsburg Institute and the NASPA/ACE Institute. Established in 1977, the Williamsburg Institute is a five-day seminar designed to assist presidents, development officers, executive directors, trustees, and others who are responsible for development and fund raising.

The National Association of Student Personnel Administrators and the American Council on Education, since 1975, have sponsored an annual institute in July for student personnel administrators. Participants include chief officers, deans, and directors of student affairs units. Themes center around the leadership and administration of student affairs in higher education. Currently headquartered at the University of Maryland, the Institute rotates around the country.

Other specialized programs exist for administrators. One example is the Summer Institute on College Admissions, jointly sponsored by Harvard University and the College Board.

Business Management Institutes

The regional associations of the National Association of College and University Business Officers (NACUBO) sponsor the College Business Management Institutes. While the best known of the three programs is co-sponsored by WACUBO (Western Association) with Stanford University, others are co-sponsored by CACUBO (Central) and the University of Nebraska at Omaha and SACUBO (Southern) with the University of Kentucky. The Eastern Association (EACUBO) offers a four-day Chief Business Officers Institute. All of the programs focus on fiscal management, administration, personnel management, higher education law, labor relations, and planning. Formats vary. The Stanford program lasts two weeks. Participants in the University of Kentucky program attend a series of one-week sessions over a three- to five-year period.

Programs for administrators of a particular type of institution

Most associations hold special conferences and seminars for administrators of its member institutions. The American Association of Community and Junior Colleges (AACJC) is particularly good at this programming, with an especially active professional development menu. For presidents alone, there are several levels of programming. Formats for these programs are similar: Each day begins with a general session in which a nationally renowned speaker introduces topics for the day. Participants pursue these topics in small groups, then report back to the entire group at the end of the day. Similar programs are available for other levels of administrators.

Programs in the liberal arts

The Troutbeck Program represents yet another category of administrative conferences. Named for the location of this annual seminar, its goal is the "intellectual renewal of academic leaders." Sponsored by the Educational Leadership Project of the Christian A. Johnson Endeavor Foundation, presidents "explore with their colleagues a series of writings in philosophy, history, and politics, and reflect upon enduring values." Through discussions, the program aims to "equip presidents to rethink and expand their vision of the academic mission, renew their sense of intellectual confidence, overcome the sense of isolation in their positions, and deepen their perception of what leadership entails." Participants are selected by the Foundation, rather than through application. Spouses are encouraged to attend and may participate in the main program. They also meet "among themselves to discuss the role of a presidential spouse." The Foundation sponsors a similar, but short, program for trustees (The Troutbeck Program 1985).

Similar programs with an emphasis on liberal arts, sponsored by such esteemed institutions as Williams College and Dartmouth College, exist for executives of business and industry.

General notes on administrative conferences

The major strength of administrative conferences lies in the opportunities for administrators to make contacts with other executives in similar situations and to discuss with these new friends the basic problems of running an educational institution. Bruce H. Leslie, a new president of Onondaga Community College and a participant in the 1984 session of "Launching

TABLE 4

AN OVERVIEW OF REPRESENTATIVE ADMINISTRATIVE CONFERENCES

Title	Sponsor	Length	Timing	Founding
Academic Leadership Institute	AASCU	5 days	Summer	1987
Business Management Institute	WACUBO, Stanford University	13 days	Summer	1975
College Business Management Institute	SACUBO, University of Kentucky	1 week sessions over 3- to 5-year period	Summer	1952
Chairing the Academic Department	ACE	1 week	Twice annually	1973
Institute for Student Personnel Administrators	NASPA and ACE	5 days	Summer	1975
Institute for Trustee Leadership	AGB	4 days	Twice annually	1985
National Conference of Academic Deans	Oklahoma State University	4 days	Summer	1941

the Presidency'' noted it was good to know ''that other people are losing as much sleep as I am'' (Heller 1984b, p. 17).

Administrative conferences address management, education, and leadership issues in proportionally smaller quantities and

Location	Size	Cost	Curriculum
Location changes annually	20	$485	Assessing Leadership Styles; Consensus Building; Linking Planning & Budgeting; Curriculum for the 21st Century; Legal Issues in Higher Education
Palo Alto, CA	55–60	$1975	Fiscal Management & Planning; Investments & Banking; Sponsored Programs; Personnel Management; Law; Labor Relations: Modeling; MIS; Taxes; Audit; Procurement
Lexington, KY	520 in 8 sections	$295, R&B extra	Roles of Officers; Organizational Structure; Financial Affairs; Personnel Administration; Business Services; Data Processing; Physical Plant; Public Safety; Auditing; Planning
Various locations	65	$375/ $450*	Role of the Chairperson; Chairperson's Roles, Powers & Responsibilities; the Department in the Context of the College; Decision Making; Performance Counseling; Dealing with Conflict & Maintaining Faculty Morale; Faculty Development; Evaluation
University of Maryland	50	$550/ $625* R&B extra	Recent themes: Partnerships (with History, Academic Affairs, the Management Team, Business & Technology, Our Future); State of the Art: The Leadership and Administration of Student Affairs in Higher Education
Various locations	30	$1100	Strengthening the Relationship between Trustee Chairperson and CEO; Responsibilities of Chair and CEO for Educating and Leading the Boards They Serve; Relationship of Leadership Team to the Board
Stillwater, OK	70	$55	Recent themes: The Economics of Higher Education; the Role of the Dean in the Search for Educational Excellence; Education in the 21st Century: The Professoriate, Curricula, and Applied Technology

with less intensity than do national institutes (see table 4). The main strengths of these conferences for new administrators

TABLE 4 (Continued)

Title	Sponsor	Length	Timing	Founding
Presidential Seminars	ACE	5 days	Summer	
Summer Institute on College Admissions	College Board, Harvard University	6 days	Summer	1960
Troutbeck Program	Christian A. Johnson Endeavor Foundation	7 days	Summer	1984
Williamsburg Development Institute	Williamsburg Development Institute	5 days	Summer	1977

R&B - Room and board
*Tuition price for members of sponsoring organization/for nonmembers

seem to be the dispensing of practical and useful advice, the offering of a framework for new knowledge, and the providing of links to other colleagues. For academic administrators with many years of experience, renewal programs offer, according to Harvey A. Stegemoeller, president of Capital University, "some privacy for thought and reflection, a bit of recreation of psyche, a few days away from burnout, weariness, and nose against the mirror all the time" (McDade 1986, p. 58).

Conventions of National Associations
Most of the national higher education associations sponsor annual or biennial conventions for members. In general, conventions have the following characteristics:

Location	Size	Cost	Curriculum
Location changes annually	35	$1000	Recent themes: Ethical and Institutional Leadership in Higher Education; The Effective CEO; The 6,000-Minute Sabbatical
Cambridge, MA	125	$650	The Search for Appropriate Admissions Practices; Managing Enrollments in the Light of Increasing Costs; Professional Growth and Personal Development; Improving the Quality of Schooling in America; Technology in Admissions
Troutbeck, NY	15	N.A.	Intellectual renewal of academic leaders through literature in philosophy, history, politics, ethics
Williams-burg, VA	125	$530	Institutional Planning; Psychology of Fund Raising; Annual Gift Programs; Major Gift Solicitation; Planned & Deferred Giving; Capital Campaigns; Managing the Development Program; Foundation & Corporate Fund Raising; Time Management

- From two to five days in length;
- Sponsored by national higher education associations;
- Held in hotels in major cities;
- Personal or institutional membership in the association usually required for participation;
- Unlimited enrollment;
- Participation generally national but rarely international;
- Follow-up available through publications and other regular association activities, although they may not be in direct support of the convention's activities and discussions;
- Administrators attend according to the type of institution and type of position, institutional support for travel, and personal interest in the association and the theme of the convention;
- Focus on higher education issues.

Conventions usually include activities and programs centered around a specific higher education issue. Recent examples of themes for the conventions of the American Association for Higher Education (AAHE) include "Taking Teaching Seriously" (1987), "Less Talk, More Action: Moving from Rhetoric to Genuine Reform" (1986), "The Undergraduate Experience: From Taking Courses to Taking Charge" (1985), "Schools and Colleges: Toward Higher Performance" (1984), and "Colleges Enter the Information Society" (1983). The theme serves as a focus for major speakers, panel discussions, lectures, workshops, round table discussions, and small group meetings.

Most conventions meet in a major city and alternate geographic areas so that all members are near a convention one year or another. Conventions last from two to five days, although many associations are adding a pre- or post-day of special interest meetings or sessions for which members can pay an additional fee. Conventions typically offer several major sessions, often with nationally prominent speakers and concurrent minor sessions. Participants attend sessions of personal interest or meetings of groups of which they are members. Pedagogy is traditional: speakers, panel discussions, position papers, and question-and-answer sessions.

The largest annual conventions are sponsored by the organizations with the broadest membership bases: the American Association of Community and Junior Colleges (AACJC) with approximately 3,500 registered participants, the American Association for Higher Education (AAHE) with approximately 1,500 to 2,000 registrants, and the American Council on Education (ACE) with approximately 1,000 participants (figures supplied by the associations). Other organizations with more specialized membership such as the National Association of State Universities and Land-Grant Colleges (NASULGC) and the Council of Independent Colleges (CIC) also host large annual conventions.

National conventions offer important educational benefits. Because conventions are planned by college and university leaders who are dealing with the pressing problems of higher education on their own campuses, the themes selected usually reflect the burning issues of concern to higher education administrators. Associations, with a promise of large audiences, are able to present nationally prominent speakers such as the Secretary of Education, presidents of large corporations or significant colleges and universities, or authors of current best-selling higher education books or studies. With so many people present, it is easy to find people from similar institutions with whom to talk and compare notes and problems. Because of the flexible organization of the sessions, a participant can attend a wide variety of presentations or concentrate on only a few. Many people stay after sessions for additional discussions, often one-on-one, with the speakers or panelists.

Houle (1980) noted that many educational techniques

> *are combined, often in complex and intricate ways, at conventions, which, because of the interaction of many stimuli, often have an impact greater than the separate effects of papers, business meetings, lectures, discussions, ceremonials, and exhibits. Conventions and other general assemblies also provide the major areas in which the mode of inquiry is conducted. Committees meet, special interest groups press their distinctive points of view, policies are debated and decided, and leaders are chosen. The conceptual and the collective identity characteristics of professionalization . . . are defined, debated, decided, and interpreted to the membership of the profession. Both instruction and inquiry modes are fostered, not only by all the processes mentioned above but also by the informal association that is a natural component of an intensive experience, which provides a continuing basis for the shop talk that shapes and reinforces opinions* (p. 202).

Because of their organization, length, and theme orientation, national conventions are strong on issue exploration and contacts but weak on the development of management skills. Administrators overwhelmingly cite the opportunities for making contacts as the true strength of the convention format. One president noted, "I've attended many conventions, but I still find the conversations more important than the sessions" (McDade 1986, p. 61). Many echo the sentiment that much of the important work of conventions actually takes place in the hotel lobbies, lounges, and restaurants after the formal sessions have ended. "A lot of the benefit of these programs is informal in the lounge," remarked Harry Jebsen, Jr., dean of arts and sciences, Capital University (McDade 1986, p. 61). In these informal settings, administrators discuss issues, compare situations, gather information, and test ideas.

The American Association for Higher Education (AAHE) offers a registration option for groups of participants attending from the same institution. In addition to reducing the cost for groups, AAHE will provide rooms for the groups to discuss the topics of the convention and arrange special meetings with convention speakers.

By participating in the activities and programs of national associations, new administrators can gain an introduction to the leaders and issues of their field. Participation provides senior administrators with the opportunity to "capitalize on the depth and breadth of their knowledge and practice" by serving as association officers, presenting papers, and moderating convention sessions (Moore and Young 1987, p. 65).

Short Seminars, Workshops, and Meetings
The vast majority of professional development programs available to both academic and nonacademic administrators of all institutions and at all position levels are seminars, workshops, and meetings. While many are advertised in national publications and attract a national audience, most are available only to administrators on a regional or state basis. In general, these programs have the following characteristics:

- From one to three days in length;
- Sponsored by a wide variety of associations, institutions, foundations, government agencies, private companies, and consulting firms;
- Located in major airline hub cities or on college campuses;
- Enrollment usually on a first-come, first-served basis;
- Participation may be national, but usually is more regional;
- Follow-up depends on sponsoring organization;
- Focus on specialized issues and problems in both the educational and management areas.

Sponsors
A major provider of short programs is the National Center for Higher Education Management Systems (NCHEMS) located in Boulder, Colorado. Historically its programs have emphasized quantitative and analytical management education. Recently

NCHEMS has been presenting more programs on planning, decision making, and consulting (Keller 1983). The NCHEMS programs are typically offered in two or three major cities, such as Atlanta, Chicago, and Boston, on alternating dates. The National Association of College and University Business Officers (NACUBO) offered a typical range of programs in 1987: "Analyzing Costs for Resource Allocation," "Enrollment or Financial Forecasting and Management," "Linking Planning with Budgeting," and "Enhancing the Academic Workplace." Like the NCHEMS programs, all of the NACUBO sessions, with the exception of the workshop on federal affairs, are held in at least two and often three locations across the country during an academic year so that administrators will not have far to travel.

In recent years the Association of Governing Boards (AGB) has become more active in producing seminars on trustee leadership. Its annual agenda includes programs on academic affairs and institutional development for trustees and senior administrators. Another new entry is the Conference on Creative Management in Higher Education sponsored by *Administrator*, the Management Newsletter for Higher Education. Topics range from "Becoming a Change Agent" and "Institutional Networking" to "Contingency Planning."

Management and leadership programs applicable to higher education administrators are available from a number of organizations that primarily serve the business community. The American Management Association (AMA) is one of the oldest and largest suppliers of management seminars and programs. AMA courses are held throughout the year and topics vary in scope from general to very specific.

The Center for Creative Leadership in Greensboro was founded in 1970 by the Smith Richardson Foundation as a nonprofit educational institution with the mission to improve the practice of management in commerce, government, education, and public service. Its training programs are designed, with the knowledge and insights gained from behavioral science research, to assess and teach leadership skills. Workshops generally use interactive techniques such as role playing, simulation exercises, and videotaped reviews. Workshop topics include leadership development, leadership education, managing for creativity, and implementing innovation. Although the programs are filled primarily by corporate clients, the Center provides scholarships (typically at 25 percent of the tuition fee) for executives of colleges and universities, especially women and minorities (Center for Creative Leadership 1987; Gardner 1987; Edgerton 1985).

The quality of instruction and leadership of workshops, seminars, and meetings can vary considerably. Many administrators prefer to take programs sponsored by well-known institutions or associations or groups of which they are members. Other administrators feel they would attend a one-day program sponsored by an unknown organization if the topic were exactly and immediately applicable to a problem at hand, but they would be reluctant to invest any more time. Commented Robert Karsten, provost of Capital University, Ohio:

> *I prefer nonprofit sponsors . . . [whose] organization [I know something about]. I watch the programs offered by these types of organizations carefully. I also pay attention to organizations with a personal track record. Once I've attended a good program from a group, I'm more inclined to try a second program* (McDade 1986, p. 65).

Formats, pedagogy, and content
The programs in this category use a wide variety of formats. Traditionally, a seminar suggests a small discussion group led by a knowledgeable teacher or practitioner. A workshop implies a laboratory situation or simulation. A meeting is generally a group of administrators of similar positions gathered to discuss topics on an agenda (Henderson 1970). But there is great variation across these types. One popular format requires teams of administrators to bring a specific institutional problem to the workshop. During the program they develop an action plan to address that problem. In another format, a particular problem is announced in advance; later all participants work as a group to explore and solve the problem.

Since these programs are quite brief, the topic for discussion is generally narrow and specific. Topics advertised for recent programs range from an examination of the new tax legislation and its implications for colleges to an introduction to quality assessment procedures. Participants usually take home specific new knowledge or skills.

Set-your-own-agenda meetings
Many administrators prefer the meetings of state or regional associations, since the agendas are set by participants them-

selves and the meetings are run by leaders of their own choosing. These types of meetings often are the most relevant to the situations on their own campuses. Robert A. Greene, provost, University of Massachusetts, Boston, described such a program, informally known as the "Urban 13" for the 13 urban institutions that participate:

It's a group of provosts and VPs of academic affairs of urban institutions. It's a unique group. It's utterly informal. There's no president, no dues. It's a group of friends. The goal is to informally share problems and solutions. There are round table discussions although we occasionally bring in a speaker on topics such as telecommunications, computer literacy. It's been extremely valuable because I've gotten to know the people so well. It's a personal network. This group has so completely filled my needs that the other types of professional meetings just don't cut it (McDade 1986, p. 65).

Michael J. Sheeran, vice president of academic affairs, Regis College, Denver, belongs to a more organized group, this one for academic officers of Jesuit colleges.

I attend meetings for corresponding officers of Jesuit schools. It's a problem-sharing session. The schools are similar enough that you get good analogous information and ideas. I usually bring back three to four workable ideas that make the price of the trip worthwhile. There's a built-in network [from this group] and that is critical. And the informality is great (McDade 1986, pp. 65–66).

General notes on seminars, workshops, and meetings
The principal benefit of these types of programs is the exposure to specific skills, problems, solutions, or issues in a short time frame. These programs usually are to the point and summarize the essential details. Such short introductions or intense, in-depth explorations of a topic are often exactly what an administrator needs to resolve a problem on his or her own campus.

The brevity of the programs can be both a blessing and an obstacle. Because these programs are short, an administrator can attend several a year without being absent from his or her office for very long. Costs, both for the programs and for travel, can be minimal. This is especially true for regional meetings that can be reached by automobile. With these factors combined, it is often possible, over the course of a year, for an administrator to attend many programs.

This brevity can also be a drawback. While a meeting or seminar may provide an excellent introduction and overview to a subject, it is often difficult to extensively explore a topic. It is even more difficult for participants to broaden their perspectives. Because of the short time frame, these programs do not provide the degree of personal contacts, networking opportunities, and sharing best found in the longer programs of national institutes and administrative conferences. Obviously, the exception is a group that meets regularly, such as Sheeran's council of Jesuit deans or Greene's "Urban 13," which usually provide an opportunity to develop significant contacts and friendships over time.

Summary
Although higher education professional development programs vary by mission, educational goals, content, intended audience, format, pedagogy, length, site, size, and sponsor, they can be compared in a number of ways. This chapter suggested a typology of four types loosely based on educational mission and goals and length: national institutes and internships; administrative conferences; conventions; and workshops, meetings, and seminars. Other useful ways to categorize programs include participants' job level, participants' functional area, and content. To find the most relevant professional development opportunities, programs should be analyzed with all these factors taken into consideration.

USES, BENEFITS, AND PROBLEMS OF PROFESSIONAL DEVELOPMENT PROGRAMS

There is general consensus in professional development literature that specific management skills can be learned or improved. To mention just a few examples, it is clear that administrators can increase their knowledge of planning models, enhance their public speaking skills, improve their effectiveness in financial management and budgeting. But there continues to be debate on whether or not critical thinking, integration, and leadership can be learned except through actual on-the-job experience that builds on natural ability.

John Gardner argues that since many "people with substantial native gifts for leadership often fail to achieve what is in them to achieve," it is "our task to develop what is naturally there but in need of cultivation" (Gardner 1987, p. 3; O'Banion 1977). The problem lies in knowing what to develop, how to develop it, and how to assess what was developed. As with education in general, and particularly a liberal arts education, it is difficult to define what professional development should be, let alone what it should achieve. Although benefits can be enumerated through anecdotal evidence, they are intensely personal and not easily quantifiable.

The problem lies in knowing what to develop, how to develop it, and how to assess what was developed.

Another problem with the evaluation of professional development is that it has diverse effects for different people at distinct points in their lives. "Leadership development," notes Gardner, "calls for repeated assessments and repeated opportunities for training" (Gardner 1987, p. 4).

The literature on the assessment of professional development programs is mostly a debate on the relative benefits claimed by programs and confirmed by anecdotal evidence of alumni and the problems enumerated by critics and participants. It is necessary to understand both the anticipated benefits and the possible drawbacks to be able to devise ways to derive the best possible experiences for both individuals and institutions.

Uses and Benefits
Curriculum content
To a great extent, an administrator chooses to attend a professional development program because of an interest in the proposed subject. Consequently, a program is evaluated based on the immediate usefulness of that content when the administrator returns to his or her job. The NCHEMS, NACUBO, and many of the ACE workshops rank high on usefulness. They are designed to present specific and tangible information on a distinct management problem or higher education issue. An ad-

ministrator who attends a seminar on "Fundamentals of Grant and Contract Management" will probably return home able to outline tasks and actions that can be executed to reap immediate rewards. But many administrators agree that "conferences are really more for enhancement than for learning basic skills. . . . The transition from the conference idea to the actual skill use is not easy. You need to have had some cursory knowledge from before" (McDade 1986, p. 83).

New ideas, stimulation, and learning

The curriculum, faculty, and participants of professional development programs are significant sources for new ideas (Andrews 1966). Professional development programs also provide the stimulation necessary for creativity and for infusing new ideas into old frameworks. Professional development programs are particularly fertile places for new ideas because participants are temporarily freed from the physical and routine restraints of their institutions. Changing structure, even if the change is only attendance at a one-day meeting, changes thinking patterns. Coupled with exposure to new ways of thinking, current theory, and subject experts, participants are often able to put pieces together in new and productive ways (Gardner 1987; Starcevich and Sykes 1980; Argyris and Cyert 1980; Levinson 1968).

While all professional development programs can provide stimulation and new ideas, many administrators find that the convention format is particularly fruitful. They like having numerous speakers presenting information on recent research or successful campus programs, because this format provides an excellent opportunity to sample many ideas in a short time. Discussion sessions and informal conversation with presenters and other participants provide another source for inspiration.

The ideas collected at professional development programs may have long-term or immediate payoffs. Harold E. Shively, former president of Bunker Hill Community College of Boston, remembered that at one conference he found out that a large company was moving into the city. "I followed up on the tip when I returned. Soon we [Bunker Hill Community College of Boston] were doing a quarter of a million dollar program for them" (McDade 1986, p. 85).

Godsey (1983) argues that because of the peculiar position of administrators in the academy, it is important that they preserve for themselves, and as a symbol for the community, their roles as learners. An administrator can suffer burnout from the daily detail and problems. Administrators, particularly the senior executives who are leading an institution, need the same stimulation of learning to do their jobs effectively as the faculty needs to pursue research and teaching. Administrators must preserve their need and right to be learners if they are to bring new ideas to their work. However, administrators' schedules rarely afford them the luxury of teaching, let alone attending, a college course. Instead, administrators can seek short, intensive learning experiences. Professional development programs provide these opportunities.

Contacts and networking

One of the primary missions of professional development programs, whether implicitly or explicitly stated in the brochure, is to provide opportunities for administrators to meet each other (Argyris and Cyert 1980). These opportunities for contacts and networking are particularly important for senior administrators, who are usually the only one of their kind on their campus. Thus, they must go outside the campus for professional assistance (Kerr 1984; Lindquist 1981; Fisher 1978).

Programs provide different types of contacts and opportunities for networking. Kanter and Wheatley (1978) identified two types of networks: "those on a national scale that create importance that can be brought home to one's institution in the form of prestige, boosting power on campus; and those that are essentially localized and provide immediate job-related exchanges" (pp. 99–100). Conventions, national institutes, and administrative conferences provide and reinforce the first type of networks, while regional and local meetings of professional associations and institution groups furnish the second.

Kanter and Wheatley found that people who share "a similar training experience do not necessarily have similar job demands" and thus rarely hold together in a network (p. 100). However, participants in professional development programs attended by administrators of similar types, levels, and responsibilities tend to develop and then maintain stronger networks for trading information, providing support, serving as another source of endorsements for jobs, and supplying professional assistance. Kanter and Wheatley (1978) found the networks of the Institute for Educational Management (IEM) and the ACE Fellows much stronger because program participants had similar job levels and responsibilities. The networks of other

programs they surveyed that had classes of mixed types and levels of administrators were weaker or nonexistent. The longer lengths of the Institute for Educational Management, ACE Fellows, and HERS programs also contributed to the strength of the networks, because participants had a longer time together during the program to form friendships and professional links.

Alumni from the ACE Fellows program and the Institute for Educational Management confirm that the friendships made during the programs continue long afterward. "A major benefit of IEM was the networks. They were more than just contacts; they were more personal," explained William J. Hynes, academic dean, Regis College, Denver, an alumnus of 1982. "We still keep in touch. I have all the names [of my classmates] on my PC. I often send things out and I get lots of correspondence back. It perpetuates and distributes a lot of good, interesting, and useful information (McDade 1986, p. 48). Suzanne Swope, an ACE Fellow in 1981–82, commented,

> *Through my experience in the Fellows Program, I have developed a network of colleagues whose support, knowledge of the field, and willingness to help have served as a resource for mutual growth. These colleagues have given me a multidimensional view of higher education which has helped me to become a better policy maker and administrator* (ACE 1987, p. 2).

The research of Kanter and Wheatley showed that networks that do not do something fall apart. It is not by chance that most of the national institutes provide official and tangible support for alumni networks. Many keep in touch with alumni through newsletters and sponsor annual events for alumni. ACE, IEM and MDP, MLE, and HERS sponsor receptions for alumni at major higher education conventions. In addition to articles on IEM's programs and faculty, the *IEM Newsletter* includes features on alumni and pages of "Class Notes," which include professional information such as job changes and publications as well as personal information such as marriages and travel of alumni.

McDade's (1986) research on the views of senior administrators on professional development showed that administrators valued more highly the contacts or networking benefits of professional development programs than issues exploration and skills benefits. They felt that all types of programs provide better contacts than skills benefits, although the balance depended on the type of program.

The development of contacts and network building requires work, but it can also be a self-fulfilling legacy. Administrators with large networks of contacts are more likely to run into others whom they already know at programs, and thus they generally feel more comfortable. From these contacts, they have a greater opportunity to meet others and to expand their number and range of contacts. Some programs increase the opportunities to develop contacts through small group discussions and meetings of participants with similar interests. One of the primary purposes of programs for new senior administrators is to provide a nucleus of contacts in the new job level.

Materials

While the content and participation of many programs is powerful for the participants, the materials from the programs can have an additional impact of their own when reviewed again at home after the program, when used as a reference long after the program, and when distributed to colleagues on campus.

Conventions often make available printed copies and tapes of speeches by key presenters. Advertisements for many seminars state that tuition price includes a manual of documentation. Many of the national institutes (IEM, MDP, HERS) provide sets of binders containing all of the reading materials for the course, which are generally later displayed in office bookshelves and referred to often. Upon his return from IEM to the University of Illinois–Chicago, Clarke Douglas, dean of students, formed "a student affairs library where student affairs journals, materials, and papers brought back from conferences [including his IEM curriculum binders] could be made available for all of the division" (*IEM Newsletter* 1987, p. 6).

Team building

Rarely is an institution led by just one leader. Usually, there is a team of leaders/managers who share the tasks and responsibilities of guiding the institution. "Each member of the team contributes to the organization's goals even though only one leader may be visible to the public" ("Expert on Leadership" 1986, p. 8). Although senior officers may be individually successful, they must function as a team to have maximum effectiveness for the institution.

One way to build a senior administrative team is through group participation in professional development programs. Many organizations provide discounts for the attendance of several administrators from the same institution. As noted, AAHE offers not only a discount but also special programming for administrative teams attending its conventions.

Several programs are specifically designed for the attendance of teams. For example, the programs for trustee development of the Association of Governing Boards are typically organized for a team of president and chair of the board of trustees or academic vice president and trustee chair of the committee on academics. Other programs are designed so that a team of administrators can focus on an institutional problem and develop plans to address that problem with the benefit of critique from the program's faculty and other participants.

National institutes provide another route to team building. Over a period of several years, the senior administrative officers of Longwood College, Virginia, and Dowling College, New York, attended the Institute for Educational Management. Although each participant developed personally, they brought back "a common vocabulary and context for discussion." According to Phyllis Mable, vice president for student affairs at Longwood, the collective experience "gave us a common vision of management. It helped to mold us into a stable and visionary team. . . .We have a common bonding." Janet Greenwood, president of Longwood during this period, explained that as a result of participating in IEM, her senior officers were able to "think institutionally. After the IEM exposure, I [could] share with my vice presidents more of the work of advocating for the institution" (*IEM Newsletter* 1987, pp. 7–8).

At the Community College of Rhode Island, Robert Silvestre, vice president for academic affairs, used materials and experiences from his participation in the Management Development Program to conduct a one-semester, in-house seminar for his staff. As a result of his MDP-based program, the "staff works better as a group now because they are more comfortable with each other and know a bit more about the functioning of each other's areas" (*IEM Newsletter* 1987, p. 6).

Time for reflection and thought
Administrators must spend so much of their time fighting "brush fires" that there is rarely time left for reflection and thought. They need time to review their goals and their prog-

ress toward those goals, to think about what they do and why, to review what others have done, and to reflect on their strengths and weaknesses (Godsey 1983; Green 1983; Eble 1978; Kanter and Wheatley 1978; Mintzberg 1975). Drucker (1973) argued that attending professional development programs is a way for executives to keep alert and mentally alive, to "get out of the trenches" (Green *Forthcoming*). Programs often provide a way "to bring enjoyment back into what has become a tedious, beleaguered, and increasingly difficult job" (Lindquist 1981). Administrators often need to physically remove themselves from their regular environment to really be able to reflect and think.

While short meetings, workshops, and conferences provide brief moments away from the job for reflection and thought, the longer programs (national institutes and administrative conferences) often include ample time in their schedules for just this purpose. Many administrators find this format allows them time to wander without agendas, to pursue an interest after a presentation by further discussion with the speaker or colleagues, or to search out a session on another topic.

Promotability

One of the most pervasive myths surrounding professional development programs is that participation in the "right" programs will increase promotability. Evidence, albeit scant, is contradictory. The literature of the national institutes contains data on the number of alumni who have moved to more senior positions since participation in the programs. The annual brochure on the ACE Fellows Program includes the latest statistics on the career moves of participants. The annual statistical profile published by HERS/Bryn Mawr contains a listing of the senior administrative positions to which alumni have recently moved.

But in reality, "the effects of such activities on career development are almost totally unknown" (Green *Forthcoming*). Jack Schuster, a long-time follower of professional development programs in higher education, commented:

Suggestions that participation in a particular program may have accelerated participants' careers [are] simply not substantiated by available data. While participants in the sought-after ACE Fellows or IEM programs may enjoy enviable promotion rates, evidence of causation is scant to nonexistent. It may well be that many of those participants had already been "fast-tracked" by their home institutions and that selection to participate merely confirms their institution's confidence that a participant is primed for advancement. . . . There is no evidence to establish that one kind of program is more efficacious than another" (Green *Forthcoming*).

Kanter and Wheatley (1978) examined five training programs that received support for the advancement of women in higher education administration from the Carnegie Corporation during the seventies. While only two (IEM and the ACE Institute) of the five programs examined in the study still exist, the results of the study may still be relevant. Kanter and Wheatley argued that professional development programs have limited success in boosting careers because the experience gained is never fully integrated into the job.

There is a striking agreement, both from individual narrations of careers and research findings, on the key elements to career success: role models, good contacts, sponsorship, visibility, being in the right place at the right time, a job that forces one to learn new skills. Training programs that occur outside of an institution are separated from these real sources of career success: the people and jobs that impede or facilitate individual careers. In some instances, training tried to offer a short-cut approach to further careers; it attempts to teach new skills, create connections among people, promote individual visibility and offer good role models. But training is an extrainstitutional response to a clearly institutional problem. As such, its impact is badly circumscribed (Kanter and Wheatley 1978, p. 58).

At best, they concluded, professional development programs provide a spurt of energy but have minimal long-term effects on careers.

Research results aside, people continue to apply to professional development programs, particularly the prestigious national institutes, with the belief that completion of the program will further their careers. The vast majority of applicants for IEM state that their career objective is to become a college president. While program participation may not catapult people into the next rung of administration, it may validate accomplishments and past experiences, test abilities, verify expectations, and certify preparedness.

Identification of new leaders

In any field there is the need to identify today the leaders for tomorrow. Instead of waiting for new leaders to emerge through natural selection, the academy needs to search for new leaders. Opening senior positions of leadership to an increasingly diverse pool of talent will accomplish this (Green 1987, 1985). Participation in professional development programs provides important access to executive administrative positions by exposing women and minorities in the first levels of senior leadership positions (such as assistant and associate vice president jobs) to the networks, broadened perspectives, and national activities of senior leadership.

This access is the specific mission of the HERS programs. Considerable time is invested during the programs in helping participants to understand their career map, the institutional world in which they function, and the processes and methods for visibility and career advancement. ACE publishes separate data on the career promotions of minority and women alumni. Most of the programs based on competitive applications emphasize that they particularly seek women and minorities. Many provide special scholarship assistance for these groups.

There is no particular study evaluating whether the access of women and minorities to senior administrative positions has increased through the attention of professional development programs. Participation, particularly in the prestigious programs, does provide a type of certification or "rite of passage" that often substitutes for administrative experiences and provides a visibility beyond one's own institution. In addition to the professional credentialing that such programs furnish, they provide important personal boosts of broadened perspectives and increased self-confidence (Green 1985; Moore 1983; Moore et al. 1983; Ernst 1982).

Despite the career advantages that participation in some programs can bring to women and minorities, Kanter and Wheatley (1978) found that some institutions sponsored women for professional development programs for less than altruistic reasons. Some institutions sent women and minorities more as a means of "showcasing" them and as evidence of the institution's supposed commitment to the promotion of women and minority candidates. Although the institutions appeared progres-

Instead of waiting for new leaders to emerge through natural selection, the academy needs to search for new leaders.

sive, the women involved felt patronized and resented that the institutions did not take advantage of their newly developed skills. In the long run, the institutions failed "to reap the benefits of [their] substantial financial investment in their training" (p. 30).

Nonetheless, many institutions use professional development programs as a formal mechanism for access. Princeton University, Ohio State University, and Iowa State University are among the many schools that have institutionwide selection processes to identify and nominate participants, principally women and minorities, to professional development programs such as national institutes and administrative conferences. Their efforts are still too new to be able to evaluate their success.

Experience enhancement
In business and government, a hierarchy of positions provides training in management techniques and experiences in leadership. But the hierarchy of higher education administration is very flat. There are only a few significant steps leading to each senior position, and each position has such distinct responsibilities that holding a job on one level does not provide sufficient training for a job on the next level. Institutions must find suitable ways for administrators to learn the management techniques and leadership skills necessary for a new job without learning through costly on-the-job mistakes (Dobbins and Stauffer 1972; Knapp 1969).

Although there is no real substitute for on-the-job learning, professional development programs provide an excellent alternative and "can be far more efficient in delivering a concentrated dose of needed information or skills" (Green 1985, p. 8; Green *Forthcoming*). A new vice president who now must devote significant time to fund raising and must become involved in an institution's lobbying relationship with state government can acquire a better understanding of the components of the job by attending a professional development program specifically targeted to these areas. Professional development programs are particularly powerful when they are chosen because of their relevance to on-the-job projects and current institutional problems.

Rapid obsolescence of experience
Irwin Miller of Yale's School of Organization and Management observed that "by the time you are in midcareer your 'experience' will have been gained in a world that no longer exists"

(Gardner 1987, p. 23). This stark comment reinforces the need for continuous professional development as a way to keep abreast of new developments, trends, and issues.

Skills learned five years ago, even two years ago, may be out of date in the light of recent technological advances or legislation. Not only is it necessary for administrators to continually add to their abilities by developing fresh skills and acquiring new leadership techniques, they also must keep going back to stay abreast of current information. An administrator needs to actively pursue professional development just to keep up, let alone to get ahead.

Improved specialization or broadened perspectives

Managers often require instruction in functional areas to learn new skills or to update skills as technology and theory change. Some professional development programs are designed to improve an administrator's areas of specialization (Rausch 1980; Lusterman 1977). For example, the Business Institutes offered by WACUBO, CACUBO, and SACUBO are particularly designed to improve the financial and business management skills of officers such as vice presidents of administration. The Williamsburg Institute explores both the management and leadership issues of institutional advancement.

Administrators, particularly at senior levels, need to be able to place their job and institution within an appropriate context. These officers

> *need opportunities to broaden their perspectives, to expand their vision beyond a particular position or institution, and to integrate new information that will help them put their work in context. The higher the level of responsibility, the greater the need to raise one's sights, to understand the interrelationship of all the parts and to place the institution in the larger social and institutional context* (Green 1987, p. 3).

Professional development programs for senior administrators, particularly national institutes and administrative conferences, are often designed with the goal of broadening participants' perspectives. When asked what was the most significant result of their participation in a professional development program, 6,000 respondents of 39 college-based professional development programs for business executives overwhelmingly replied, "The program broadened me" (Andrews 1966, p. 162).

This broadening can be in many areas. First, professional development programs provide an opportunity to scan the environment, to explore external trends, events, and activities in other fields and at other institutions. A senior administrator will be better able to place his or her institution in its communities, to anticipate future problems, and to take advantage of forecasted trends and events.

Second, professional development programs provide an opportunity to better understand the activities of other areas of the institution and the world in which administrators lead, while preparing administrators for a more complex role or a completely different position in an institution (Peck 1984; Rausch 1980). This is a broadening both in a general understanding of the world in which an administrator must work and in the skills an administrator uses to function effectively in that wider arena. In a survey of the top executives of Phillips Petroleum, 80 percent felt that the general purpose of a professional development program was to broaden the participant's view about the managerial function (Starcevich and Sykes 1980). Kanter and Wheatley (1978) found that "the variety of participants—from institutions different by size and type—allows one to hear different perspectives on similar problems, and also to learn that many problems are not unique to one's own dilemmas" (p. 19).

This broader perspective generally enables the administrator to make decisions that involve the entire institution and its environment. Higher education administrators need to keep abreast of the new and complex higher education issues so they can adjust their actions to them (Campanella et al. 1981; Fisher 1978a; Newell 1978; Levinson 1968).

Learning as renewal

Warren Bennis contends that leaders value learning and mastery (1984). Leaders find the learning experience to be invigorating and exhilarating. This is probably particularly true for the leaders of colleges and universities. Many of these senior administrators began as teachers, researchers, and scholars. They elected careers in academe because they enjoy working in an environment charged with the electricity of learning. They chose their jobs because learning is both professionally and personally interesting and important to them.

Although a love and need for learning may be an important characteristic of senior executives of colleges and universities, formal, planned, and organized learning often fills only the smallest percentage of their work lives. Instead, they spend their days fielding phone calls, sitting in meetings, attending ceremonial events, keeping appointments, and solving problems, both big and small. Although these tasks may all be learning experiences in their own ways, this constant rush of activity leaves little time to systematically explore a subject or to thoroughly survey new issues. In short, the officers who organize the academy so that others may learn in the most effective fashion often have the least opportunity to pursue formal and organized learning for themselves. And yet, it is this type of orderly and planned learning that is often the most fulfilling and renewing for an administrator. The act of learning can bring "a fresh and discerning eye to bear upon even the most routine situation, . . . but to the extent that there is failure to do so, learning dries up at its freshest and most fruitful source" (Houle 1980, p. 45).

The very act of once again being a student in an educational setting may be one of the most important aspects of attending professional development programs. While it is, of course, important to learn *something*, it is just as significant, simply, *to learn*, to explore, to question, to search. This process of learning can provide an energy that can permeate unrelated areas of job performance long after the program itself is completed.

Increased self-confidence

Just as learning can increase satisfaction and energize performance, so it can bolster self-confidence. Since many of the senior executives of colleges and universities backed into administration after initial careers in other fields, few have had actual training in management and even fewer have had any type of leadership education. Attending a professional development program on technical topics or on leadership techniques can demystify subjects so they can be mastered. And mastery leads to self-confidence.

Kanter and Wheatley (1978) found that as a result of participation in professional development programs, 67 percent of the sample "had become importantly aware of new skills and abilities . . . including the ability to think strategically, to analyze problems and create strategies for addressing them" (p. 32). Increased self-confidence and a more clearly defined image of skills and abilities can have an important impact because such an image can alter behavior (p. 59).

When alumni of national institutes discuss their experiences, one of the most common themes is the self-confidence they gained and the belief that they are as good, if not better, than others at administering their institutions. Participants come to understand their competitive strengths and how best to use them. They better analyze their weaknesses and what they must do to grow in those areas. With increased self-confidence, an executive may be more willing to tackle new problems and projects and more comfortable with the roles and responsibilities of administration and leadership.

Problems
Career timing
There is both a right time and a wrong time for certain types of professional development. The benefits of a program can be completely lost if the administrator is not in the right career and experience stage. Lindquist (1981) argued that professional development is in essence adult development. Professional development experiences should be chosen not only for their content but also for the match of program goals and format to the maturation stage of the administrator.

There is a growing body of research on the developmental stages of adulthood (see the work of Levinson and Erickson). This literature suggests that there is a series of definable periods, each different, through which adults pass. These phases are the result of

> the response to specific social and psychological tasks. . . .
> As such, development is not simply a consequence of aging.
> Instead, development is seen as the qualitative change in a
> person's meaning system (Kegan and Lahey 1984, pp. 200,
> 202).

Hodgkinson's research (1981, 1974) on the stages of adult development is relevant when matching professional development programs to career evolution and personal maturation.

Hodgkinson found that, during their twenties, administrators are just beginning in the world of management and need to explore the details of their specialization area. They need courses on management basics and programs that will help them further understand their specialization areas. Workshops, short seminars, and meetings that focus on the area of specialization while introducing management skills perhaps best meet these needs. During this period administrators begin to attend their professional associations' conventions and start to investigate the issues of their field and their relationship to the total institution. By attending professional development programs, they begin to develop contacts to form a network of colleagues in their field. Hodgkinson noted that a neophyte administrator during this period of career development is further behind in his or her career maturation than a faculty member of similar age. Because faculty members launch their careers even as graduate students, through research for a dissertation and practice teaching as section leaders or teaching assistants, they generally have more real experience before their first academic appointment than do administrators, who usually do not start managing until their first job.

An administrator in his or her thirties is finding a niche, becoming one's own person, and is trying (often successfully) to win a first major administrative position. This administrator needs more management courses with extensive forays into leadership techniques and programs that will begin to broaden his or her perspectives on the home institution and its environment. Internships, such as the ACE Fellows, are particularly useful during this phase because they provide intensive exploration of administration and its role in higher education institutions. Many professional associations provide special programs for "new administrators," those in their first substantial management position in the field. The NASPA/ACE Institute in student personnel is a good example. During this period administrators begin to attend conventions of associations for institutional groups such as the Council of Independent Colleges. One way of "Becoming One's Own Person," a theme of this phase, is by developing a reliable circle of professional friends at other institutions both for job contacts and for knowledge of impending issues and problems. National institutes and administrative conferences are particularly helpful in developing this type of network, while conventions are of assistance in tending and maintaining such a network.

Hodgkinson described the period roughly between 39 and 43 years of age as "middlescence," when administrators must adjust dreams to the realities of their career choices. This is the period that separates the "rising stars" who will continue on their way to the senior positions from those who remain in middle-level positions. Both types need programs to further broaden their perspectives and to better understand the institution in its entirety. They need more exposure to management skills as they encounter new problems and to leadership techniques as they encounter new challenges. They also need additional time for reflection on both institutional and personal goals. The range of program possibilities for this group is endless. National institutes and administrative conferences serve both groups.

This period also holds the greatest threat of burnout. Participating in professional development programs may offer an important release for these feelings as well as the boost of energy, enthusiasm, and ideas necessary for recharging (Green 1987). It is no coincidence that many of the conferences that attract administrators in this career phase are in resort areas and include substantial time for relaxation and reinvigoration.

Hodgkinson termed the period between 43 and 50 years as "restabilization." During this time, administrators accept life as it is, establish new personal goals, acknowledge the institution for what it is, and realistically settle on the true impact that they can make in the academy. Like earlier phases, this phase can profit from professional development programs that will continue to refine management skills and leadership techniques.

Kegan and Lahey (1984) noted that during this period adults lessen their identification with their jobs and careers. An adult "may find himself wanting to place work in some bigger context that would allow him more access to a side of himself that has been neglected in the efforts of the preceding decade to establish himself" (pp. 200–201). From a study of leaders of a nationally acclaimed public school system, they determined that during this developmental period, the current feelings of leaders "seemed not so much about changes in the intensity of their commitment but reevaluations of the shape of that commitment" (p. 201). Unlike earlier phases, administrators more seriously feel the need to find opportunities where they can step out of the demands of their daily jobs and responsibilities to reflect and think. This is the period during which administrators most strongly seek "additive" educational opportunities where they can "replenish their own commitment and knowledge through lifelong learning" (Moore and Young 1987, p. 21).

It is this restabilization period that propels many long-time senior administrators and presidents with years in the job, a string of accomplishments, and a regional or even national reputation to attend a national institute such as the Institute for Educational Management or the College Management Program. Such programs provide an opportunity to ponder leadership style, to reframe the vision for the institution, and to contemplate the nature of the academy and its relationship to society in a fast-paced style with intellectual rigor that is exhilarating and invigorating, albeit mentally and physically exhausting.

Many executives during this phase find that they derive particular personal and professional benefits from serving as a mentor, for example, for an ACE Fellow. The process of teaching another about administration and leadership provides unique opportunities for reflection and reexamination of roles and responsibilities.

Unfortunately, matching the type of professional development experience to career or even personal developmental needs is rarely a consideration when an administrator chooses to attend a program. Nor do many institutions pay attention to this issue as attendance of professional development programs in negotiated. Many excellent learning opportunities are bungled or bypassed because of poor planning in this area. For example, an administrator suffering from burnout would be ill-suited to the fast-paced, intellectual boot camp atmosphere of the Institute for Educational Management. Instead, he or she needs a professional development opportunity with time for reflection, rest, and escape from the daily routine. A new president with years of experience in a vice presidential role may not need much additional exposure to higher education issues or management theory but will benefit most from seminars on leadership techniques or opportunities to broaden his or her contacts in the more general world of higher education.

Administrators consider career timing to be the most crucial factor when contemplating participation in national institutes and the second most important consideration after costs when surveying administrative conferences (McDade 1986). Because an administrator may attend an administrative conference only every few years and a national institute only once in a career, it is important that the nature and goals of the program match the developmental needs of the administrator.

Family responsibilities

Administrators must also consider family responsibilities. At times, even a day or two away can cause a hardship for families. Participation in longer programs requires detailed planning

Administrators consider career timing to be the most crucial factor when contemplating participation in national institutes and the second most important consideration after costs when surveying administrative conferences.

for care of children and, as our society ages, for parents and older relatives.

Women, particularly single mothers, find it more difficult than men to be absent for long times because of the problems of arranging for child care. The child care costs of a single mother who recently participated in the Management Development Program were almost as much as the program's tuition. Based on expectation of these problems, many women choose not to attend these programs. While most institutions pay for their senior administrators to attend professional development programs, few provide supplemental funds to cover the costs of extended child care.

Time and money

Participation in professional development programs represents an investment of time and money for both the administrator and the institution. Although it may be possible to calculate the true costs of attendance at a one-day program—the tuition price, travel expenses, and salary for the time away from work and the time needed to make up the missed work—such a calculation becomes more involved with programs of longer duration. Expenses for a senior administrator's attendance at an administrative conference or national institute do not include charges for someone to cover an additional job or factor in for opportunities lost and projects postponed.

The most important factor to an administrator when selecting a program is its curriculum. But even if the topic, format, pedagogy, and faculty are right, the cost, location, and accessibility may force him or her to skip the opportunity. In McDade's survey (1986) of the issues affecting program selection by senior administrators, cost, location, and accessibility were of the greatest importance, after content and faculty, when considering participation in conferences and conventions but least important when contemplating attendance at seminars and workshops. For these latter programs, comfort—opportunities for rest and relaxation and the presence of familiar colleagues—was the most important consideration. According to Roger Iddings, dean of the College of Education at Wright State University:

My interest is piqued by the topic because of links with problems that I'm working on. After that, what attracts me

depends on the time it is offered, my time, and my budget
(McDade 1986, p. 101).

Financial sponsorship of senior administrators to professional development programs is another important issue. While it may be expected that colleges and universities assume the costs for their participation, they do not or can not always do so. Often professional development is one of the first items cut when budgets are tight (Green 1987). Because the benefits of professional development programs cannot be easily quantified, it is difficult to argue for such funds on technical merits during the budget process.

Professional development for senior executives poses another set of problems. Because of the special nature and requirements of these senior programs (longer length, faculty of the highest reputation, more comfortable accommodations, specialized curriculum often created especially for a specific program), tuition is often greater than the costs of programs for middle managers or for faculty. Poorer colleges and universities simply cannot afford the costs of the national institutes. They find it impossible to commit several thousand dollars to a single administrator when all of the institution's administrators want and need professional development opportunities. Too often, the senior administrators of such institutions cannot consider the more expensive programs. Other institutions try to bridge this financial gap by paying part of the tuition or by attempting to find external funding through scholarships and grants.

Train 'em and lose 'em

An argument against sending administrators to professional development programs is based on the belief that after an institution invests time, energy, and money through development, the executive will move on to another institution. This argument is particularly valid for administrators moving from middle-level positions to lower senior positions (such as a dean moving to an assistant or associate vice presidency) or administrators moving from lower senior to top senior positions (such as assistant and associate vice president to vice president). The hierarchy of colleges and universities, with its limited opportunities for advancement, forces administrators to move on to another institution in order to move up.

This movement, though, puts professional development in disfavor. Instead, it may be more productive to think of professional development programs as a way of providing new opportunities and challenges for administrators within current jobs.

Selection, integration, evaluation, and feedback

Most institutions have no overall plan for the professional development of any of their administrators. Although middle-level administrators may be selected to attend programs within a plan set by their supervisors, there is no one but the president to direct the professional development of senior administrators. (And who guides the professional development of the president?) Instead, most senior administrators attend programs that seem worthwhile to them, fit in their schedules, and do not cost more than their travel and training budgets.

John Gardner (1987) stresses that professional development must be "linked to some form of instruction or counseling and feedback" (p. 16). Again, this may occur for middle-level administrators but rarely exists for senior administrators. However, some institutions do make attempts to organize selection, integration, evaluation, and feedback linked to participation in professional development programs.

Cornell University is one of the best examples of an institution with an integrated plan. Each winter a list of professional development programs (predominantly national institutes and administrative conferences) is circulated among middle- and senior-level administrators. Candidates petition directly to an institutional selection committee, and supervisors nominate candidates. The selection committee, comprised of officers such as the provost and the personnel director, matches candidates and programs to best address the developmental needs of candidates and to meet the future leadership needs of the institution. Once selected, the Cornell candidates must still apply to the programs for acceptance, but they are assured of Cornell's financial support and endorsement.

Candidates chosen for participation in professional development programs then complete a number of preparatory steps. As a group they meet with various officers of the university for a brief overview of the university's operations. They complete a survey to gather information on Cornell. The personnel office sponsors a reception for new candidates to meet with alumni of the programs so they can gather information and advice on the best ways to benefit from them. After the administrators return from the programs, they meet with the personnel office and their immediate supervisors. The university tries to ascertain the benefits of the programs for the individuals and whether it should continue sending participants to the programs (Atcheson 1987).

As well organized as this plan is, it still does not include methods for combining participation in professional development programs with a project back on campus, nor does it provide for opportunities to integrate new skills and abilities into real job experiences. It is most effective for middle-level and first-tier senior administrators, but it does not as thoroughly engage or serve the top executive team.

Other sources of learning
People learn in different ways. In fact, by the time one reaches adulthood, a preferred mode of learning is usually well entrenched.

An administrator typically learns in many ways and from many sources. In unpublished data from McDade's 1986 study of senior administrators' views of professional development experiences, survey participants were asked to rank their preferred way of learning new management skills and leadership techniques. They indicated that learning on the job and reading books, articles, and journals were their preferred methods. Attending programs and asking colleagues were third and fourth on the list.

It is not surprising that reading was such a strongly favored mode of learning. As discussed in the chapter on the career paths of senior administrators, most began their work as professors. Their roots are in scholarship and their training is in research, critical reading, and analytic writing. They remain the preferred learning modes even after the administrator has left the faculty.

McDade's research (1986) showed that intentional administrators, those who planned and worked toward a career in administration, use a greater variety of sources of information to improve their performance and to better execute their responsibilities. They just as often acquire information by asking colleagues, attending seminars, workshops, and institutes, and even enrolling in academic courses as they do by reading. These administrators seem to be particularly enthusiastic about participating in specialized administrative conferences for senior administrators or attending higher education conventions.

Unintentional administrators, those who had not planned a career in administration, rely much more heavily on the traditional learning style of reading. Interviews to explore the meaning of these statistics revealed that unintentional administrators most often are looking for short-term information to accomplish the job at hand. Because they define their administrative stint as a short-term break from other responsibilities (usually academic), they define their needs for information, management skills, and leadership techniques in terms of the present job and its problems, but not in terms of the long-term needs of the institution, higher education, or their own careers. Their long-term visions are framed by the context of their "real" career, usually as a teacher, researcher, and scholar. While contact with other executives is helpful, they see their real networks among the colleagues of their discipline.

Because intentional administrators frame their careers within the context of management, they tend to place the problems and challenges of their current job in the context of a career in administration. Thus, they more often attempt to learn through a variety of methods that will elicit not only information for the present but contacts and networks in management for the present and the future.

Job coverage and the backed-up work on the desk
One of the biggest complaints of participants about attending professional development programs concerns the work that greets them upon returning to their office. Several late nights of work may be required to catch up on the work missed while attending even a one-day seminar. The problem compounds with the length of the program.

While it may be possible to postpone, or arrange for someone else to cover, the responsibilities of a middle-level administrator while he or she is away, such arrangements are not as easily accomplished for senior administrators. Because of the institutionwide and "end-of-the-line" responsibilities of the job, it is often impossible to postpone work or to arrange for someone else to cover. Planning attendance at a professional development program requires careful coordination with other members of the senior executive team to anticipate problems, arrange supervision of routine tasks, and prepare contingency plans for the unexpected. While a senior administrator at a large institution may be able to temporarily delegate work and responsibilities to associate and assistant vice presidents, such delegation is particularly difficult at a small institution where the senior team may include only four to six people.

Extended time away from the job is especially difficult for a president. There is no "good" time to leave the institution no matter how valuable and beneficial participation in a program may be. While a president is expected to travel a great deal as the representative of the institution, the people back on the campus still expect the president to be there when they need or want him or her. If one of the other senior administrators is asked to substitute, there is still the problem of coverage for that administrator's work and responsibilities.

Many of the longer professional development programs are scheduled in the summer when the responsibilities of senior administrators are less pressing and more easily postponed. Nonetheless, many participants still try to take their jobs with them to the programs. They are the participants who use the pay phone in the lobby between each session to call the office for an update on activities. But it is impossible to derive the fullest benefits of a professional development program, particularly the benefits of a break from routine and a fresh perspective on problems, if the daily details of the job are still present.

Summary

While there is strong anecdotal evidence that professional development programs provide important benefits, there is little quantitative evidence to support their value. The short-term gains of content and skills can be lost if not immediately applied to job-related problems and projects, yet few participants or institutions plan for post-program evaluation or implementation. Although the long-term benefits, particularly in leadership techniques, may be the most powerful, they are also the most vague and personal and therefore the most difficult to justify.

These ambiguous benefits must always be balanced against the very real problems of participation. At times, it is difficult for administrators to see beyond them. Thus, participation in professional development programs is often eliminated even before the specifics of the program are investigated.

Yet the evidence that does exist on the benefits—anecdotal, tentative, and personal as it may be—still outweighs the disadvantages tied to participation by many senior administrators.

CONCLUSIONS AND RECOMMENDATIONS

While most institutions endorse the concept of professional development for their administrators, few approach it in a way that truly provides the maximum benefit for individual or institution. Usually a senior administrator will choose a program without guidance or coordination with other members of the senior team. Often the only criterion that will matter is that the total costs of professional development programs not exceed the amount assigned in the yearly budget. "A systematic approach to leadership development can also assist institutions in making better use of the funds allocated for this purpose and achieve a greater return on their investment" (Green 1987, p. 2).

The women administrators interviewed by Kanter and Wheatley (1978) for their study on the impact of various professional development programs commented that the programs they had attended were "a great personal experience," yet few of their institutions had used their newly developed skills (p. 11). Their experiences were not atypical. They represent perhaps the greatest problem with professional development programs for all levels of administrators and the greatest loss for both individuals and institutions. Most administrators attend programs in a vacuum with little attention from colleagues and supervisors and with virtually no integration into the institutional plan.

Most administrators attend programs in a vacuum with little attention from colleagues or supervisors and with virtually no integration into the institutional plan.

To derive the greatest benefit from the professional development of personnel—faculty, staff, and administrators—institutions must set institutional goals and an integrating plan. There must be planning and follow-through by administrators, supervisors, and other members of the senior executive team, including the president and the board of trustees who ultimately monitor the performance of the institution's administrators.

The Role of Trustees in Supporting
Professional Development

It is ultimately the responsibility of a board of trustees to review the overall governance of its institution and to create an effective environment for leadership. By monitoring and evaluating the performance of each member of the senior administrative team, the board would be better able to support management and leadership improvement. Such prescriptive evaluations of senior officers by boards of trustees could strengthen the leadership, and thus the governance and structure, of the entire institution.

Each individual's evaluation should include an examination of job performance and a determination of salary recognition. It should also include an analysis of the individual's management skills and leadership techniques and judge how up to date they are and how relevant to the institution's projects and problems. It may be helpful to measure performance by comparing the job requirements against a theoretical list of senior administrative responsibilities and skills instead of a job description. The earlier list of skills and knowledge necessary for administration or the lists provided by any number of writers on leadership (Gardner 1986; Bennis 1984) may serve as the launching point for a more creative analysis.

Together, the board (or its evaluation team) and the senior officers should plan ways for each to address areas of less expertise and experience. While Kerr's report specifically addressed the issue of strengthening presidential leadership, the charge to the board is also applicable to the entire senior leadership team. They

> *should be encouraged to take advantage of opportunities for professional development (as part of working time) through travel abroad and attendance at conferences, seminars, and summer training sessions. Attendance at association meetings with other [senior administrators] can often be not only an excellent learning experience but also very refreshing as [senior officers] share their problems, and in hearing, lighten their sense of burden* (Kerr 1984, p. 48).

Members of boards of trustees are chosen, in large part, for their experiences and expertise in management and leadership, which, it is hoped, they will share with the institution. Most work in business and industry where professional development is a normal, routine, and expected part of all managers' lives. Often, trustees are alumni of university executive development programs, active in their own professional associations, or teaching in programs in their own industry. They shape and direct professional development policies for their own companies yet neglect to apply the same guidelines to the higher education institutions they advise.

Trustees can better create a prescriptive evaluation process by requiring not only a job performance review, but an assessment of management and leadership abilities as well. Such an appraisal could be completed by an outside evaluator, collected through interviews with members of the senior team and their subordinates, or compiled through the self-analysis of each officer. The board or the evaluation committee should discuss the results of this assessment with each officer to determine major goals for management improvement and professional development participation. While it is inappropriate for a board to become involved in the decision of who attends each and every conference, convention, or seminar, it is the responsibility of the board to encourage or even require senior officers to regularly participate in major learning experiences. To this end, the board (or its evaluation team) should become familiar with the major types of professional development opportunities available and discuss options with the senior officers.

When a board and a senior officer agree on the officer's participation in a major professional development program, the board should ensure that the officer is truly free of the day-to-day responsibilities of his or her job. Programs such as the Institute for Educational Management, HERS/Bryn Mawr, and the College Management Program require that participants be officially relieved of responsibilities for the duration of the program and that someone else be assigned temporarily. This should guarantee that the participant will not be bothered by job-related phone calls and mailed materials or required to return home during the program. Such interruptions violate the learning environment of the program, diminish the officer's ability to concentrate and wholly participate, and reduce the total learning experience.

Upon completion of a major professional development experience or as part of an annual job performance review, senior officers should summarize what they learned at the program(s) and how applicable it is to their job and the institution. They should then evaluate the quality of the actual programs. The summary will provide a basis for future job appraisal, while the evaluation will help the board to assess whether it wants to continue sponsoring participation in particular programs.

It is difficult for the president and members of his or her leadership team to declare professional development for senior administrators as an institutional goal since they would become major beneficiaries of the policy. Instead, it may be more politic for the board of trustees to issue a statement of policy and to back it with tangible support of money and personal involvement. The board should do whatever is necessary to institutionalize professional development so that all levels of personnel—faculty, staff, and administrators—can benefit.

*Boards must recognize that even in tight fiscal times, ex-
penditures on professional development by the president and
others will improve the performance of administrators on
many fronts. While knowledge and skills acquired through
seminars and workshops can have a clear pay-off in terms of
money saved and lawsuits headed off, the personal renewal
of administrators will also accrue benefits to the health and
vitality of the institution* (Green *Forthcoming*).

A Role for Foundations in Professional Development

Most of the major professional development programs for administrators of higher education were created with funds from
foundations and corporations. Once the programs became established, most of the foundations moved on to support other projects, leaving the programs to be self-sufficient. The financial
base for these programs consists of tuition, fees, and contribu-
tions from alumni. Occasionally, program expenses are aug-
mented by grants for supporting research solicited by program
director(s).

This self-sufficiency covers the costs for the programs.
Rarely are substantial funds left over for curriculum research
and design or for more theoretical research in the developmental needs of administrators or the future issues of higher education institutions. By investing in professional development
programs, foundations could make a significant difference in
. the current and future leadership of colleges and universities.
Funds are needed in three areas:

- Additional research is needed to support the development
  of management and leadership expertise. Some areas include adult development as it applies to career evolution
  and learning theory and styles. Also needed is research
  into the career paths of higher education administrators,
  emphasizing experience building and skill development.
- Even successful programs need periodic evaluation and
  redesign, no matter how great the costs. Funds are needed
  to assess the current and future educational needs of
  senior administrators and to develop curriculum materials
  relevant to their management and leadership situations.
  More professors need to be trained in the teaching techniques used at executive programs, such as case teaching,
  role playing, and simulation, which are often very different from the techniques used by professors in graduate and

undergraduate classes or even by speakers at conventions and meetings.

- Although senior officers and boards of trustees may agree that professional development opportunities can be beneficial, many institutions simply cannot spare the funds. Scholarships are needed to support professional development for administrative officers of financially struggling institutions and for women and minorities. These funds could be made available in a variety of ways: directly to institutions to develop their own officers; directly to the professional development programs to subsidize tuition costs for specific groups of participants; and directly to the individuals, through national, regional, or local competitions.

Better Ways to Use Professional Development Programs

The value of professional development programs can be enhanced by preparation and follow-through. While many of these suggestions may be obvious and simplistic, few administrators make the time for them, and few colleges and universities institutionalize the procedures. The following suggestions are loosely based on the work of Van Auken and Ireland (1980).

- Before attending a program, an administrator should do some research, even if cursory, to best understand the curriculum. This will provide a better framework for understanding the particular program and will allow the participant to ask more informed questions. Even if the program addresses a problem currently facing the administrator, he or she can list the key aspects of the problem and the areas that would most benefit from assistance.
- An administrator should discuss the goals, content, and format of the program with colleagues. There may be topics that, although not immediately interesting or applicable to the participant, may be of great interest to the other administrators of the institution. By attending those sessions and reporting back to colleagues, benefits can accrue to more than just the participant.
- Some programs have unique pedagogy or formats. This is particularly true of national institutes and administrative conferences. It is helpful to obtain a list of past participants, particularly those from the last year or two, and ask them questions about the program. What did the alumni

feel were the strengths and weaknesses of the program? In hindsight, what could the alumni have done on his or her own to mitigate the weaknesses? Would particular preparations have made the program more productive? What is the best advice for deriving the most value from the structure, the content, the other participants, the faculty?

- Before leaving for the program, it is important to determine the best way to document information. Notes will be most helpful if they are organized by their intended use. While taking notes during programs high in content may be relatively easy, it is more difficult to document programs that concentrate on process and experiential learning. Through the years, participants in the Institute for Educational Management have used a variety of techniques to capture these more intangible insights. Some keep journals in which they discuss new insights and fresh ideas. One recent participant wrote a letter to himself at the end of each day so he could collect observations. When he returned home the letters were a welcome reminder and a detailed record of his experiences. Another participant, perhaps more bold, sent similar letters to his assistant. Each letter contained notes, an outline, or action that the administrator planned to take based on an experience or conversation that day. By sending the letters, the administrator guaranteed that his goals were on record and that, in a public way, he was committed to the actions. Other participants have taken notes in several colors: one color for content, another color for new ideas and insights, another color for future actions.

- It is smart to plan opportunities to meet colleagues at professional development programs. Because of their large attendance, conventions provide a prime opportunity to meet with other administrators to discuss specific problems and issues, especially if appointments are made beforehand. It is easier to see a number of people at a convention than to travel to meet each one individually. Often, associations will confirm if someone is registered or send out early versions of registration lists. It is not unusual to see administrators at the convention registration line first checking the listings of participants at the back of the program brochure before reading the listings of program sessions at the front of the brochure.

- After attending the program, it is helpful to report to

colleagues on the experience and to critique benefits, shortcomings, and overall impact. Materials should be distributed. A report should be written that summarizes insights and discoveries. Such a report should evaluate the program and include an action plan for developing the ideas gathered there. Even if the program was a one-day meeting of professional colleagues, it is best to take notes on the meeting for later reference. These notes and reports should be reviewed periodically to recapture insights, to evaluate progress on plans, to measure performance and development, to remember contacts, and to survey needs for future professional development.

Van Auken and Ireland (1980) argued that professional development programs

are a major source of human resources investment . . . [and] like any business investment, a satisfactory return must be sought despite the subjective and qualitative nature of seminar learning. Only through designing and implementing a seminar investment strategy . . . can returns be maximized (p. 21).

Professional Development of Middle-Level Administrators
As Scott (1978b) observed, "Higher education has not yet realized its responsibility for the professional development of its mid-level staffs" (p. 28). Professional development for middle-level administrators is in the same disorganized state as that of senior-level executives. While the same type of programs exist for them, the numbers of programs vary. There are fewer national institutes and administrative conferences for middle-level administrators.

If the research on the roles and responsibilities of senior administrators has been moderate, comparable research on middle-level administrators has been minimal. Since it is nearly impossible to ascertain the professional development needs of middle-level administrators without first understanding what they do and how they contribute to the institution and its mission, few development programs have been developed for this group. The national professional development programs are more likely to be pegged for "beginning administrators" rather than for middle-level executives. Or programs for conventions or professional associations are generic, with a little bit of something for everyone who attends.

Institutions with strong professional development plans usually include both middle and senior executive groups. For example, while Longwood College uses the Institute for Educational Management for team building among senior administrators, it uses the Management Development Program and HERS/ Bryn Mawr for the development of middle-level managers. The Cornell program encourages both senior- and middle-level administrators by endorsing a range of programs with a wide range of applicability.

Future Research Agendas
Since the organization and sponsorship of professional development programs are so decentralized, it is unlikely that the results of research will greatly influence the design and structure of programs already in existence (Green *Forthcoming*). Yet over time older programs have changed as sponsors refined and further tested their content, pedagogy, and format. Research may have its most significant impact on the development of new programs. It may influence how individuals and institutions use professional development programs.

The literature of adult development is growing steadily and has already produced many insights into career evolution and professionalization. Although the research of Hodgkinson, Kegan, and Lehay and others in adult development has important application to the understanding of administrative growth, there is a need for more research with specific orientation to the development of management expertise and leadership style. How do the challenges of management and leadership mesh with the maturation of adults, with their growth needs, and with their psychological evolution? With increased application of these theories of adult, career, management, and leadership development, institutions will be better able to understand and prepare for the education of their key administrators. Research in this field will benefit not just higher education, but business, industry, government, and the military.

Further research into the career paths of academic and non-academic administrators will also help us understand their professional development needs. As we better appreciate the varied experiences of administrators, it will be easier to plan ways to fill in experiences, reinforce abilities, and develop skills. It will be helpful to better understand what administrators do, what they need to know to perform their jobs, and what they desire to learn to better fulfill their responsibilities (Green *Forthcoming*; Moore et al. 1983; Hodgkinson 1981, 1974).

The literature on learning styles is already substantial. Much has been written on the theories of adult learning styles as they apply to continuing and professional education. We need to further elaborate the theories of learning styles for the areas of management skills and leadership techniques.

There is a strong literature on continuing professional education derived from experience in the fields of medicine, dentistry, accounting, law, library science, and finance (Houle 1980). The literature addresses such issues as the best ways to fortify learning after returning to work, the most beneficial forms of on-the-job and in-house education, and the best methods for professional development for groups and individuals. One of the issues not sufficiently explored involves the true costs of professional development. While the literature can help institutions invest in professional development for their administrators, there is still a need for more specific research in leadership education.

Although many programs collect data on their effectiveness (as defined by the program), career enhancement of alumni, and other program attributes, there has been virtually no in-depth and comprehensive research on the benefits and effectiveness of professional development for senior or, for that matter, any level of administrators. The Kanter and Wheatley study (1978) focused on only eight programs (only two are still in existence) and how they affected women participants. McDade's study examined only the tangible benefits of content and contacts. The study by Andrews (1966) is still the most encyclopedic survey of professional development programs, but it considered only business programs and their effect on business executives and the study is now more than 20 years old.

To better design programs, we need to know what can best be taught in this format and what impact participation in various types of programs has on the skills and abilities of administrators. In short, we need to know what works and what does not work. Does participation in major professional development programs make a difference in career development? Does such participation improve the access of women and minorities to senior administrative positions? The answers to these questions would have a significant impact on the policy decisions of administrators choosing programs, on the way institutions plan for the development of their administrators, and on the foundations and associations that provide the major funding for many programs (Green *Forthcoming*; McDade 1986).

Despite the minimal amount of concrete documentation available to substantiate how these programs aid in the refinement of skills, exploration of issues, and advancement of careers, these programs provide a vital means of administrative and leadership development that should not be ignored or neglected.

APPENDIX

NAMES AND ADDRESSES OF REPRESENTATIVE PROGRAMS

American Association for Higher Education (AAHE)
One Dupont Circle, N.W., Suite 600
Washington, DC 20036
(202) 293-6440
Contact: Ann Ford

American Association of State Colleges and Universities (AASCU)
Academic Affairs Resource Center
One Dupont Circle, N.W., Suite 700
Washington, DC 20036
(202) 293-7070
Contact: Evelyn Hively

American Association of Community and Junior Colleges (AACJC)
One Dupont Circle, N.W., Suite 410
Washington, DC 20036
(202) 293-7050
Contact: Connie Odems

American Conference of Academic Deans
Association of American Colleges (AAC)
1818 R Street, N.W.
Washington, DC 20009
(202) 387-3760
Contact: Shelagh Casey

American Council on Education (ACE)
Center for Leadership Development
One Dupont Circle, N.W., Suite 800
Washington, DC 20036-1193

Fellows Program
(202) 939-9420
Contact: Madeleine F. Green

Chairing the Academic Department
Workshop for Department/Division Chairpersons
(202) 939-9415
Contact: Rose-Marie Oster

Presidential Seminars
(202) 939-9410
Contact: Marlene Ross

Association of Governing Boards of Universities and Colleges (AGB)
One Dupont Circle, N.W., Suite 400
Washington, DC 20036
(202) 296-8400
Contact: Barbara Taylor

American Management Association (AMA)
135 West 50th Street
New York, NY 10020
(212) 903-8040

AMA Extension Institute
P.O. Box 1026
Saranac Lake, NY 12983

Business Management Institute (National Association of College and University Business Officers)
CACUBO
University of Wisconsin/Milwaukee
(219) 844-0520
Contact: Gary Newsom

SACUBO
6 Blazer Hall
University of Kentucky
Lexington, KY 40506-0012
(606) 257-6368
Contact: Kathy Hatfield

WACUBO
P.O. Box 2349
Stanford, CA 94305
(415) 642-8292
Contact: Stephanie Siri

Center for Creative Leadership
5000 Laurinda Drive
P.O. Box P-1
Greensboro, NC 27402-1660
(919) 288-7210
Contact: Patricia A. Wegner

College Management Program (CMP)
Carnegie-Mellon University
School of Urban and Public Affairs

Schenley Park
Pittsburgh, PA 15213-3890
(412) 268-2195
Contact: Harry Faulk

Creative Management in Higher Education
6401 Odana Road
Madison, WI 53719
(608) 273-0350 and (800) 233-9767
Contact: Gudrun Sindermann

Institute for Educational Management (IEM)
Harvard University
339 Gutman Library, Appian Way
Cambridge, MA 02138
(617) 495-2655
Contact: Sharon A. McDade

Institute for the Management of Lifelong Education (MLE)
Harvard University
339 Gutman Library, Appian Way
Cambridge, MA 02138
(617) 495-3572
Contact: Clifford Baden

Management Development Program (MDP)
Harvard University
339 Gutman Library, Appian Way
Cambridge, MA 02138
(617) 495-2655
Contact: Sharon A. McDade

Management Institute for Women in Higher Education (HERS/ New England)
Higher Education Resource Services
Wellesley College
Wellesley, MA 02181
(617) 235-0320, x2529
Contact: Susan Knowles

National Association of College and University Business Officers (NACUBO)
One Dupont Circle, N.W., Suite 510
Washington, D.C. 20036
(202) 861-2500
Contact: Mary Beth Holm

**National Association for Student Personnel Administrators/
American Council on Education (NASPA/ACE) Institute for
Student Personnel**
> University of Maryland
> 2130 North Administration
> College Park, MD 20742
> (301) 454-2925
> Contact: William L. Thomas, Jr.

**National Center for Higher Education Management Systems
(NCHEMS)**
> NCHEMS Management Services, Inc.
> P.O. Drawer P
> Boulder, CO 80302
> (303) 497-0365/0345
> Contact: Grace Morlock

National Conference of Academic Deans
> EAHED
> 309 Gundersen Hall
> Oklahoma State University
> Stillwater, OK 74078-0146
> (405) 624-7244
> Contact: Thomas Karman or John Gardiner

**Summer Institute for Women in Higher Education Administration
(HERS/Bryn Mawr)**
> For information about admissions process and residential living:
> Bryn Mawr College
> Bryn Mawr, PA 19010
> (215) 645-6161
> Contact: Margaret M. Healy

> For information about curriculum, faculty, and alumnae activities:
> HERS, Mid-America
> Colorado Women's College Campus
> University of Denver
> Denver, CO 80220
> (303) 871-6866
> Contact: Cynthia Secor

Summer Institute on College Admissions
> 4 Clematis Road
> Lexington, MA 02173
> (617) 492-6573
> Contact: Jacquelyn R. Smith

The Troutbeck Program
      The Educational Leadership Project
      The Christian A. Johnson Endeavor Foundation
      109 East 89th Street
      New York, NY 10128
      (212) 534-2904
      Contact: Nicholas Farnham

Williamsburg Development Institute
      109 Crownpoint Road
      Williamsburg, VA 23185
      (804) 220-7155
      Contact: Roger Thaler

RESOURCES ON PROFESSIONAL DEVELOPMENT

Bricker's International Directory
      Bricker Executive Education Service
      Peterson's Guides, Inc.
      166 Bunn Drive
      P.O. Box 2123
      Princeton, NJ 08543-2123

An Independent Sector Resource Directory of Education and Training Opportunities and Other Services
      Independent Sector
      1828 L Street, N.W.
      Washington, D.C. 20036

REFERENCES

The Educational Resources Information Center (ERIC) Clearinghouse on Higher Education abstracts and indexes the current literature on higher education for inclusion in ERIC's data base and announcement in ERIC's monthly bibliographic journal, *Resources in Education* (RIE). Most of these publications are available through the ERIC Document Reproduction Service (EDRS). For publications cited in this bibliography that are available from EDRS, ordering number and price are included. Readers who wish to order a publication should write to the ERIC Document Reproduction Service, 3900 Wheeler Avenue, Alexandria, Virginia 22304. (Phone orders with VISA or MasterCard are taken at 800/227-ERIC or 703/823-0500.) When ordering, please specify the document (ED) number. Documents are available as noted in microfiche (MF) and paper copy (PC). Because prices are subject to change, it is advisable to check the latest issue of *Resources in Education* for current cost based on the number of pages in the publication.

Books and Articles

Allen, Louise H. Summer 1984. "On Being a Vice President for Academic Affairs." *Journal of NAWDAC* 47(4): 8–15.

Andrews, Kenneth R. 1966. *The Effectiveness of University Management Development Programs*. Boston: Division of Research, Graduate School of Business Administration, Harvard University.

Argyris, Chris, and Cyert, Richard M. 1980. *Leadership in the '80s: Essays on Higher Education*. Cambridge: Institute for Educational Management, Harvard University. ED 215 609. 96 pp. MF–$1.04; PC not available from EDRS.

Atwell, Robert H., and Green, Madeleine F., eds. December 1981. *Academic Leaders as Managers*. New Directions for Higher Education No. 36. San Francisco: Jossey-Bass.

Barnard, Chester I. 1968. *The Functions of the Executive*. Cambridge: Harvard University Press, 1968.

Bennis, Warren. August 1984. "The Four Competencies of Leadership." *Training and Development Journal* 38(12): 15–19.

Billy, Christopher, ed. 1987. *Bricker's International Directory: University Executive Programs*. Princeton: Peterson's Guides.

Birnbaum, Robert. May 1983. "Searching for a Leader." *AAHE Bulletin* 35(9): 9–11.

Blake, Robert R.; Mouton, Jane Srygley; and Williams, Martha Shipe. 1981. *The Academic Administrative Grid*. San Francisco: Jossey-Bass.

Blyn, Martin R., and Zoerner, C.E., Jr. March 1982. "The Academic String Pushers: The Origins of the Upcoming Crisis in the Management of Academia." *Change* 14(3): 21–25, 60.

Bolman, Frederick W., Jr. 1964. "Can We Prepare Better College and University Administrators?" *Current Issues in Higher Education*. Washington, D.C.: American Association for Higher Education.

Bolt, James F. November/December 1985. "Tailor Executive Development to Strategy." *Harvard Business Review* 64: 168–76.

———. Winter 1987. "The Future Is Already Here." *New-Management* 43: 27–29.

Bray, Howard. April 1987. "Getting Fiscal in Academe." *Across the Board: The Conference Board Magazine* 24(4): 53–56.

"Bricker's Bulletin on Executive Education." Fall 1986. Vol. V. Princeton: Bricker Executive Education Service.

———. Spring 1987a. Vol. VI. Princeton: Bricker Executive Education Service.

———. Summer 1987b. Vol. VI. Princeton: Bricker Executive Education Service.

Campanella, Frank F.; Keyes, Raymond F.; and Sullivan, Leo V. April 1981. *Management Development for Colleges and Universities*. Boston: Boston College.

Clement, Ronald W. Winter 1981. "Evaluating the Effectiveness of Management Training: Progress during the 1970's and Prospects for the 1980's." *Human Resource Management* 20(4): 8–13.

Creager, John A. 1966. "Evaluation and Selection in the 1966–67 Academic Administration Internship Program." *ACE Research Reports* 1(3): 1–26.

———. February 1971a. "Evaluation and Selection of Academic Interns: 1967–1968." *ACE Research Reports* 6(2): 1–25.

———. 1971b. "Goals and Achievements of the ACE Internship Program in Academic Administration." *ACE Research Reports* 6(3): 1–46.

Cross, K. Patricia. 1981. *Adults as Learners*. San Francisco: Jossey-Bass.

Cunningham, Luvern L.; Hack, Walter G; and Nystrand, Raphael O., eds. 1977. *Educational Administration: The Developing Decades*. Proceedings of a Career Development Conference Sponsored by the University Council for Educational Administration and The Ohio State University. Berkeley: McCutchan Publishing Co.

Digman, Lester A. July/August 1980. "Management Development: Needs & Practices." *Personnel* 56(6): 45–57.

Dobbins, Charles G., and Stauffer, Thomas M. Fall 1972. "Academic Administrators—Born or Made?" *Educational Record* 53(4): 293–99.

Dobrynski, Judith H. December 14, 1987. "GE's Training Camp: An 'Outward Bound' for Managers." *Business Week* 3030: 98.

Dodds, H. W. 1962. *The Academic President—Educator or Caretaker?* New York: McGraw-Hill.

Dressel, Paul L. 1981. *Administrative Leadership*. San Francisco: Jossey-Bass.

Drucker, Peter. 1973. *Management*. New York: Harper & Row.

Durea, Jerry. April 1981. "Presidents' Views on Current and Future Issues in Higher Education." *Phi Delta Kappan* 62(8): 586–88.

Eble, Kenneth E. 1978. *The Art of Administration*. San Francisco: Jossey-Bass.

Edgerton, Russ. April 1985. "News & Information: Memo to Members from Russ Edgerton." *AAHE Bulletin* 37(8): 14.

Enarson, Harold. 1962. "The Academic Vice President or Dean." In *Administrators in Higher Education: Their Functions and Coordination*, edited by Gerald P. Burns. New York: Harper and Brothers.

Ernst, Richard J. Summer 1982. "Women in Higher Education Leadership Positions—It Doesn't Happen by Accident." *Journal of the College and University Personnel Association* 33(2): 19–22.

Eurich, Nell P. 1985. *Corporate Classrooms*. Carnegie Foundation Special Report. Lawrenceville, New Jersey: The Carnegie Foundation for the Advancement of Teaching and Princeton University Press. ED 264 785. 172 pp. MF–$1.04; PC not available from EDRS.

Ewing, David W. 1964. *The Managerial Mind*. London: Collier-Macmillan Ltd.

"Expert on Leadership Discusses Who's at the Top." December 12, 1986. *Higher Education and National Affairs*. Washington, D.C.: American Council on Education.

Farson, Richard. Winter 1987. "The Electronic Classroom." *New-Management* 43: 42–44.

Fisher, Charles F. June 1977. "The Evaluation and Development of College and University Administrators. Part Two: Professional Development of Administrators." *ERIC/Higher Education Research Currents*. ED 139 363. 5 pp. MF–$1.04; PC–$3.85.

———. ed. 1978. *Developing and Evaluating Administrative Leadership*. New Directions for Higher Education No. 22. San Francisco: Jossey-Bass.

Fisher, James L. 1984. *Power of the Presidency*. New York: American Council on Education and Macmillan Publishing Co.

Fiske, Edward B. 28 January 1985. "Booming Corporate Education Efforts Rival College Programs, Study Says." *New York Times*.

Fresina, Anthony J., et al. 1986. *Executive Education in Corporate America: A Report on Practices and Trends in 300 Leading Companies in Eight Major Industries*. Palatine, Illinois: Anthony J. Fresina & Associates.

Fullerton, Gail, and Ellner, Carolyn. March 1978. "Career Patterns of Men and Women in Graduate Administration." Paper presented at the Annual Meeting of the American Educational Research Association, Toronto, Canada. ED 159 952. 23 pp. MF–$1.04; PC–$3.85.

Gaff, Sally Shake; Festa, Conrad; and Gaff, Jerry G. 1978. *Professional Development: A Guide to Resources*. New York: Change Magazine Press.

Gardner, John W. March 1986. "The Tasks of Leadership." Washington, D.C.: Independent Sector.

————. June 1987. "Leadership Development." Washington, D.C.: Independent Sector.

Godsey, Kirby R. March/April 1983. "Administrator as Learner." *Journal of Higher Education* 54(2): 193–97.

Golde, Roger A. Winter 1987. "Management Training: Get Serious." *NewManagement* 43: 30–33.

Gray, Sandra Trice. 1987. *An Independent Sector Resource Directory of Education and Training Opportunities and Other Services*. 2d ed. Washington, D.C.: Independent Sector.

Green, Madeleine F. March/April 1983. "Review of *Administrative Leadership: Effective and Responsive Decision Making in Higher Education.*" *Journal of Higher Education* 54(2): 209–12.

————. November 1985. "Discussion Paper: A Framework for Leadership Development." Photocopied. Washington, D.C.: American Council on Education.

————. 18 May 1987. "Professional Development: Expanding Human Resources in Colleges and Universities." Second Draft. Washington, D.C.: American Council on Education.

————, ed. *Forthcoming. Leaders for a New Era: Strategies for Higher Education*. New York: Macmillan.

Green, Madeleine F., and Chibucos, Thomas R. January 1987. *ACE Fellows Program: An Assessment of the First Eighteen Years*. Washington, D.C.: American Council on Education.

Greiner, Larry E. Winter 1987. "Confessions of an Executive Educator." *NewManagement* 43: 34–38.

Harder, Martha B. September 1983. "Career Patterns of Chief Student Personnel Administrators." *Journal of College Student Personnel* 24(5): 443–48.

Heller, Scott. 27 June 1984a. "Guidelines for New College Presidents: Getting Started Is No Simple Matter." *Chronicle of Higher Education*: 15–18.

————. 5 December 1984b. "American Council Fellowships: Some Say They've Replaced the 'Old Boy Network.' " *Chronicle of Higher Education*: 31–32.

Henderson, Algo D. 1970. *Training University Administrators: A Programme Guide*. Paris: UNESCO.

Higher Education Management Institute. 1978. *Management Development and Training Program for Colleges and Universities: Program Handbook*. Rev. ed. Knoxville: Higher Education Management Institute, University of Tennessee. ED 159 946. 93 pp. MF–$1.04; PC–$10.13.

Hodgkinson, Harold L. Fall 1974. "Adult Development: Implications for Faculty and Administrators." *Educational Record* (55)4: 263–74.

——. 1981. "Administrative Development." In *The Modern American College: Responding to the New Realities of Diverse Students and a Changing Society*, edited by Arthur W. Chickering et al. San Francisco: Jossey-Bass.

Hornig, Lilli S. March 1978. "HERStory." *Grants Magazine* 1(1): 36–42.

Houle, Cyril O. 1980. *Continuing Learning in the Professions*. San Francisco: Jossey-Bass.

Ingols, Cynthia A. 1986. "Executive Education Programs: Meeting Strategic Organizational Purposes." Doctoral dissertation, Harvard University.

Ironside, Ellen M. October 1981. "Uncommon Women/Common Themes: Career Paths of Upper-Level Women Administrators in Higher Education Institutions." Paper presented at the Joint Conference of the Southern Association for Institutional Research, Charlotte, North Carolina. ED 212 218. 22 pp. MF–$1.04; PC–$3.85.

——. March 1983. "Women as Administrators in Higher Education: Qualitative Data for Value Questions." Paper presented at the Annual Meeting of the Association for the Study of Higher Education, Washington, DC. ED 232 553. 37 pp. MF–$1.04; PC–$5.82.

Kanter, Rosabeth Moss, Wheatley, Margaret, et al. 31 May 1978. "Career Development for Women in Academic Administration: The Role of Training. A Report to the Carnegie Corporation of New York." Photocopied. Cambridge, Massachusetts: Goodmeasure.

Kauffman, Joseph F. May/June 1982. "The College Presidency—Yesterday and Today." *Change* 14(3): 12–19.

Kegan, Robert, and Lahey, Lisa Laskow. 1984. "Adult Leadership and Adult Development: A Constructivist View." In *Leadership: Multidisciplinary Perspectives*, edited by B. Kellerman. Englewood Cliffs, New Jersey: Prentice-Hall.

Keller, George. 1983. *Academic Strategy: The Management Revolution in American Higher Education*. Baltimore: The Johns Hopkins University Press.

Kerr, Clark. 1984. *Strengthening Leadership in Colleges and Universities: A Report of the Commission on Strengthening Presidential Leadership*. Washington, D.C.: The Association of Governing Boards of Universities and Colleges.

Knapp, David C. Winter 1969. "Management: Intruder in the Academic Dust." *Educational Record* 50(1): 55–59.

Knox, Alan B. 1977. *Adult Development and Learning*. San Francisco: Jossey-Bass.

Kroger, Bill. 26 March 1984. "ACE Fellows Do Well on Administrative Climb." *Higher Education and National Affairs: Newsletter of the American Council on Education* 33(5): 1, 5.

Levinson, Harry. 1968. *The Exceptional Executive: A Psychological Conception*. Cambridge: Harvard University Press.

Lindquist, Jack. 1981. "Professional Development." In *The Modern American College: Responding to the New Realities of Diverse Students and a Changing Society*, edited by Arthur W. Chickering et al. San Francisco: Jossey-Bass.

Livingston, J. Sterling. January/February 1971. "Myth of the Well-Educated Manager." *Harvard Business Review* 49: 79–89.

Lunsford, Larry W. Summer 1984. "Chief Student Affairs Officer: The Ladder to the Top." *NASPA Journal* 22(1): 48–56.

Lusterman, Seymour. 1977. *Education in Industry*. New York: The Conference Board.

———. 1986. *Trends in Corporate Education and Training*. New York: The Conference Board.

Lutz, Frank W., and Ferrante, Reynolds. 1972. *Emergent Practices in the Continuing Education of School Administrators*. Columbus, Ohio: University Council for Education Administration.

McDade, Sharon A. Spring 1984. "Report on Interviews with IEM Alumni." Photocopied. Cambridge: Institute for Educational Management, Harvard University.

———. 1986. "Professional Development of Senior-Level Administrators of Colleges and Universities." Doctoral dissertation, Harvard University.

McDonough-Rogers, Eileen; Frawley, Betsy Pingree; Sullivan, William J.; and Fairweather, Peter. 1982a. *New York: Statewide Action Plan for Management Development, Report on Pilot Surveys*. Prepared for the Human Resources Advisory Committee of the Governor's Management Task Force. Cambridge: Kennedy School of Government, Harvard University.

———. 1982b. *New York: Statewide Action Plan for Management Development, Final Report of the Executive and Managerial Development Project*. Prepared for the Human Resources Advisory Committee of the Governor's Management Task Force. Cambridge: Kennedy School of Government, Harvard University.

Main, Jeremy. 3 May 1982. "The Executive Yearn to Learn." *Fortune* 105: 234–48.

———. 28 September 1987. "Wanted: Leaders Who Can Make a Difference." *Fortune* 116: 92–102.

Mayhew, Lewis B., ed. 1974. *Educational Leadership and Declining Enrollments*. Berkeley: McCutchan Publishing Co.

Millet, John D. 1976. *The Multiple Roles of College and University Presidents*. Office of Leadership Development in Higher Education. Occasional Paper. Washington, D.C.: American Council on Education.

Mintzberg, Henry. July/August 1975. "The Manager's Job: Folklore and Fact." *Harvard Business Review* 76: 49–61.

Moore, Kathryn M. May 1983. "Administrative Careers." *AAHE Bulletin* 35(9): 5.

——. Fall 1984. "The Structure of Administrative Careers: A Prose Poem in Four Parts." *Review of Higher Education* 8(1): 1–13.

——, et al. January 1985. "Today's Academic Leaders: A National Study of Administrators in Community and Junior Colleges." University Park: Center for the Study of Higher Education, Pennsylvania State University. ED 264 922. 153 pp. MF–$1.04; PC–$16.46.

Moore, Kathryn M., and Sagaria, Mary Ann D. September/October 1982. "Differential Job Change and Stability Among Academic Administrators." *Journal of Higher Education* 53(5): 501–13.

Moore, Kathryn M.; Salimbene Ann M.; Marlier, Joyce D.; and Bragg, Stephen M. September/October 1983. "The Structure of Presidents' and Deans' Careers." *Journal of Higher Education* 54(5): 500–515.

Moore, Leila V., and Young, Robert B., eds. 1987. *Expanding Opportunities for Professional Education*. New Directions for Student Services No. 37. San Francisco: Jossey-Bass.

Mortimer, Kenneth P., and McConnell, T. R. 1978. *Sharing Authority Effectively*. San Francisco: Jossey-Bass.

Nash, Nancy S., and Hawthorne, Elizabeth M. 1987. *Formal Recognition of Employer-Sponsored Instruction: Conflict and Collegiality in Postsecondary Education*. ASHE-ERIC Higher Education Report 3. Washington, D.C.: Association for the Study of Higher Education. ED 286 437. 132 pp. MF–$1.04; PC–$14.52.

Newell, Clarence A. 1978. *Human Behavior in Educational Administration*. Englewood Cliffs, New Jersey: Prentice-Hall.

O'Banion, Terry, ed. Autumn 1977. *Developing Staff Potential*. New Directions for Community Colleges No. 19. San Francisco: Jossey-Bass.

Ostroth, D. David; Efrid, Frances D.; and Lerman, Lewis S. September 1984. "Career Patterns of Chief Student Affairs Officers." *Journal of College Student Personnel* 25(5): 443–47.

Peck, Robert D. March/April 1984. "Entrepreneurship as a Significant Factor in Successful Adaptation." *Journal of Higher Education* 55(2): 268–85.

Poskozim, Paul S. October 1984. "New Administrators—A Statistical Look at Movement within the Ranks, 1982–83." *Change* 16(7): 55–59.

Rausch, Erwin. 1980. *Management in Institutions of Higher Learning*. Lexington, Massachusetts: Lexington Books, D.C. Heath.

Richman, Barry M., and Farmer, Richard N. 1974. *Leadership, Goals, and Power in Higher Education: A Contingency and Open Systems Approach for Effective Management*. San Francisco: Jossey-Bass.

Rickard, Scott T. Spring 1985. "Career Pathways of Chief Student

Affairs Officers: Making Room at the Top for Females and Minorities." *NASPA Journal* 22(4): 52–60.

Roach, J. H. L. Winter 1976. "The Academic Department Chairperson: Functions and Responsibilities." *Educational Record* 57(1): 13–23.

Schrader, Albert W. March/April 1985. "How Companies Use University-Based Executive Development Programs." *Business Horizons* 28(2): 53–62.

Schwartz, Robert. Winter 1987. "Training for the 21st Century." *NewManagement* 43: 45–48.

Scott, Robert A. 1978a. *Development of Competence: Administrative Needs and Training Goals in American Higher Education*. New York: Exxon Education Foundation. ED 179 143. 45 pp. MF–$1.04; PC–$5.82.

————. 1978b. *Lords, Squires, and Yeomen: Collegiate Middle Managers and Their Organizations*. AAHE-ERIC Higher Education Research Report No. 7. Washington, D.C.: American Association for Higher Education. ED 165 641. 83 pp. MF–$1.04; PC–$10.13.

Short, Alice. Winter 1987. "Are We Getting Our Money's Worth?" *NewManagement* 43: 23–26.

Socolow, D. J. May 1978. "How Administrators Get Their Jobs." *Change* 10(5): 42–43, 54.

Sonnenfeld, Jeffrey A. 1983. "Education at Work: Demystifying the Magic of Training." In *Human Resource Management: Trends and Challenges*, edited by Richard E. Walton and Paul R. Lawrence. Cambridge: Harvard University Business School Press.

Sonnenfeld, Jeffrey A., and Ingols, Cynthia A. Autumn 1986. "Working Knowledge: Charting a New Course for Training." *Organizational Dynamics* 15(2): 63–79.

Starcevich, Matt M., and Sykes, J. Arnold. 1980. "Internal Advanced Management Programs for Executive Development: A Survey and Case Study." *Human Resource Planning* 3(3): 97–109.

Stauffer, Thomas M. June 1975. *Assessment of Outcomes from the Academic Administration Internship Program, 1965–1975*. Washington, D.C.: American Council on Education.

Tichy, Noel M. Winter 1987. "Training as a Lever for Change." *NewManagement* 43: 39–41.

Tinsley, Adrian. Fall 1985. "Upward Mobility for Women Administrators." *Journal of NAWDAC* 49(1): 3–11.

Twombly, Susan B. 1986a. "Career Lines of Top-Level Two-Year College Administrators: Implications for Leadership in a New Era." Paper presented at the Annual Meeting of the Association for the Study of Higher Education, 20–23 February 1986, San Antonio, Texas. ED 268 884. 34 pp. MF–$1.04; PC not available from EDRS.

———. 1986b. "Theoretical Approaches to the Study of Career Mobility: Applications to Administrative Career Mobility in Colleges and Universities." Paper presented at the 67th Annual Meeting of the American Educational Research Association, 16–29 April 1986, San Francisco. ED 271 548. 54 pp. MF–$1.04; PC–$7.76.

Ulmer, Walter. 3 June 1987. Presentation to the National Leadership Group of the American Council on Education. Washington, D.C.

Van Auken, Philip M., and Ireland, R. Diane. October 1980. "How Small Businesses Can Gain the Most from Employee Seminars." *Journal of Small Business Management* 18(4): 18–21.

Watkins, Beverly T. 13 April 1983. "Higher Education Now Big Business for Big Business." *Chronicle of Higher Education*: 1, 6.

Whetten, David A. November/December 1984. "Effective Administrators: Good Management on the College Campus." *Change* 16(8): 38–43.

Williams, Lea E. Fall 1986. "Chief Academic Officers at Black Colleges and Universities: A Comparison by Gender." *Journal of Negro Education* 55(4): 443–52.

Materials from Professional Development Programs

American Council on Education (ACE). 1987a. "The ACE Fellows Program, 1987–88." Program Brochure. Washington, D.C.: American Council on Education.

———. July 1987. "Fact Sheet: Career Paths of ACE Fellows." Washington, D.C.: American Council on Education.

American Management Association (AMA). 1987. "Make It Happen: The 1987 Self-Study Curriculum Guide." New York: American Management Association.

Bryn Mawr College and HERS, Mid-America. 1987. "Summer Institute for Women in Higher Education Administration." Program Brochure. Bryn Mawr, Pennsylvania: Bryn Mawr College and HERS, Mid-America.

———. 1987. "Participant Profile: 1987–88 Management Institute." Bryn Mawr, Pennsylvania: Bryn Mawr College and HERS, Mid-America.

Center for Creative Leadership. 1987. "Programs: January–December 1987." Greensboro, North Carolina: Center for Creative Leadership.

College Management Program (CMP). 1987. "Send the Boss Back to School." Program Brochure. Pittsburgh, Pennsylvania: Carnegie-Mellon University.

Conference of Academic Deans. 1987. "The Economics of Higher Education." Program Brochure. Stillwater: Oklahoma State University.

Institute for Educational Management (IEM). 1987a. "Profile of the

Classes 1982–1987.'' Photocopied. Cambridge: Institute for Educational Management, Harvard University.

―――. 1987b. Program Brochure. Cambridge: Institute for Educational Management, Harvard University.

Institute for the Management of Lifelong Education (MLE). 1987. Program Brochure. Cambridge: Institute for the Management of Lifelong Education, Harvard University.

Karman, Thomas A. 1 December 1983. "The Stillwater Conference." (Enclosure in a letter from Thomas A. Karman.) Photocopied.

Karman, Thomas A., and Gardiner, John. July 1985. "Thirty-ninth Annual National Conference of Academic Deans: Education for the 21st Century: The Professoriate, Curricula, and Applied Technology." Stillwater: Oklahoma State University.

Management Development Program (MDP). 1987a. "Profile of the Classes of 1986–1987." Photocopied. Cambridge: Institute for Educational Management, Harvard University.

―――. 1987b. Program Brochure. Cambridge: Institute for Educational Management, Harvard University.

Management of Lifelong Education. 1987. Program Brochure. Cambridge: Institute for the Management of Lifelong Education, Harvard University.

"The Troutbeck Program: Seminars for Intellectual Renewal of Academic Leaders." 1985. Photocopied. New York: The Christian A. Johnson Endeavor Foundation.

"Using the IEM and MDP Experience after You Return to Campus." Spring 1987. *IEM Newsletter* 3(1): 6.

Wellesley College and HERS, New England. 1987. "Management Institute for Women in Higher Education." Program Brochure. Wellesley, Massachusetts: Wellesley College and HERS, New England.

Western Association of College and University Business Officers. 1987. "WACUBO Business Management Institute." Program Brochure. Stanford, California: WACUBO Business Management Institute.

INDEX

A

AAC (see Association of American Colleges)

AACJC (see American Association of Community and Junior Colleges)

AACSB (see American Assembly of Collegiate Schools of Business)

AAHE (see American Association for Higher Education)

AASCU (see American Association of State Colleges and Universitites)

"Academic Leadership Institute" seminar, 45

Access to senior positions, 37–38, 67, 68

ACE (see American Council on Education)

ACE Fellows program, 35–37, 41, 61, 62, 65, 73, 75

Administrative conferences
       characteristics, 41–44
       examples, 44–54
       goals, 69
       overview, 48–51
       strengths, 49–50, 73, 74

Administrator newsletter, 55

Administrators
       academic, 1–4, 34, 38, 44–46
       career experiences, 5–6
       developmental stages, 72–75
       entry positions, 5
       intentional, 80
       nonacademic, 4–6, 34, 38, 46
       professional development, 8–10
       professorial roots, 2–3
       responsibilities, 11–15
       skills, 15–19
       unintentional, 80

Admissions officers: summer institute, 46

Adult development, 72–75, 90

Advanced Executive Program (Northwestern), 40

Advanced Management Course (GE), 25

Advanced Management Development Program (Boston U.), 40

Advanced Management Program (Harvard) (AMP), 26, 40

AGB (see Association of Governing Boards)

Air Force, U.S., 26

Alumni
       networking, 41, 62, 78
       promotability, 65

AMA (see American Management Association)

American Assembly of Collegiate Schools of Business (AACSB), 45

C

CACUBO (see Central Association of College and University Business Officers)
California State University system internships, 36
Canada, 29
Careers
       mobility, 1
       paths, 1–10, 90
       timing, 72–75
Carnegie Corporation, 66
Carnegie-Mellon University, 39
Center for Army Leadership, 26
Center for Creative Leadership, 55
Center for Leadership Development (ACE), 44–45
Central Association of College and University Business Officers (CACUBO), 46, 69
"Chairing the Academic Department" seminar, 45
Chief Business Officers Institute, 46
Child care issues, 76
Christian A. Johnson Endeavor Foundation, 47
Chronicle of Higher Education, 33
CIC (see Council of Independent Colleges)
CMP (see College Management Program)
Coast Guard, U.S., 26
Collaborative programs, 28
College Board, 38, 46
College Business Management Institutes, 46
College Management Program (CMP), 38–39, 75, 85
Columbia University, 27
Commercial vendors, 28
Communication skills, 15
Community College of Rhode Island, 64
Community colleges
       administrator career paths, 2
       collaborative programs, 28
       seminars, 47
Compensatory education, 23
Competitive readiness, 24
Computer science programs, 29, 38
Conference on Creative Management in Higher Education, 55
Conferences (see Administrative conferences)
Consensus development, 12–13
Consulting, 7
Contacts (see also Networking), 60–63
Control Data, 22
Conventions

J

Jebsen, Harry, Jr., 53
Jesuit colleges, 57
Job coverage/backup, 80–81, 85
Johnson and Johnson, 26

K

Karsten, Robert, 55
Keller, George, 39

L

"Launching the Presidency" seminar, 47–48
"Leaders in Transition" study, 1
Leadership courses, 26, 28
"Leadership Skills for Executives" course, 28
Learning styles, 79–80, 91
Leslie, Bruce H., 47
Liberal arts programs, 47
Lifelong learning, 23
Longwood College, 64, 90

M

M.S. in Administration, 29
M.S. in Financial Services Management, 29
M.S. in Management, 29
Mable, Phyllis, 64
Management development (see Professional development)
Management Development Programs (MDP), 38, 40, 62, 63, 64, 76, 90
Management education
      distribution, 21–22
      executive programs, 25–31
"Manager's Guide to Financial Analysis" course, 28
McDonald's Hamburger University, 26
Massachusetts Institute of Technology, 26, 27
Master's degree programs, 29
MDP (see Management Development Programs)
Meetings (see also Conventions), 54–58
Mentoring, 36–37, 75
Middle management, 17, 38, 89–90
Military
      mandatory management education, 22
      professional development, 8, 21
Miller, Irwin, 68
Millet, John D. (see also "Techniques of leadership"), 39

Minority groups
>participation, 37–38, 67, 68
>placement, 36
>scholarships, 55

MLE (see Institute for the Management of Lifelong Education)
Mobility/attrition, 77–78
Moore, Kathryn M. (see "Leaders in Transition" study)
"Moral Leadership in Higher Education" seminar, 45
Morale development, 15
"Multinational Marketing Management" program, 29

N

NACUBO (see National Association of College and University
>Business Officers)
NASPA (see National Association of Student Personnel
>Administrators)
NASPA/ACE Institute, 46, 73
NASULGC (see National Association of State Universities and Land
>Grant Colleges)
National Association of College and University Business Officers
>(NACUBO), 46, 55, 59
National Association of Life Underwriters, 29
National Association of State Universities and Land Grant Colleges
>(NASULGC), 52
National Association of Student Personnel Administrators (NASPA),
>46
National associations (see Conventions; specific associations)
National Center for Higher Education Management Systems
>(NCHEMS), 54–55, 59
National Conference of Academic Deans, 44
National institutes/internships
>alumni, 41
>characteristics, 33, 35–37
>curricula, 40–41
>examples, 35–40
>goals, 69
>intended audience, 34
>networking, 41, 73
>overview, 42–43
Naval War College, 26
NCHEMS (see National Center for Higher Education Management
>Systems)
Networking, 41, 47, 57
>benefits, 74
>opportunities, 61–63, 73, 88
"New Deans Seminar", 45

New England Telephone's Learning Center, 26
Niagara Institute, 29
Northwestern University, 27, 40
NTL Institute, 28

O
"Occupational career" building, 9
Ohio State University, 68
Oklahoma State University, 44
Orientation programs, 23

P
Pennsylvania State University, 27
Perlman, Daniel H., 36
Phillips Petroleum, 70
Planning needs, 12, 19
Policy
    corporate seminars, 24
    development, 85
Presidents
    administrative conferences, 44–45, 47
    backup, 81
    career paths, 2, 3, 7
    participants, 37
    placement, 35
    professional development interests, 19
Princeton University, 68
Problems
    attrition, 77–78
    career timing, 72–75
    family, 76
    job coverage, 80–81
    learning modes, 79–80
    selection/integration/evaluation/feedback, 78–79
    time/money, 76–77
Proctor and Gamble, 26
Professional associations, 7
Professional development
    analysis of needs, 11
    definitions/objectives, 59
    implications, 8–10
    most frequent needs, 18
    problems, 72–81
    rate of participation, 7
    recommendations, 87–89
    sources and types, 25–30

T

Teaching experience, 2, 5, 6
Team building, 63–64
"Techniques of leadership," 12, 13, 15, 16
Texas A&M University, 45
Texas Instruments, 22
Time constraints, 64–65, 76–77
Training (see Corporate education; Professional development)
Troutbeck Program, 47
Trustees
       role, 83–85
       seminars, 45, 47

U

U.S. Army, 23, 26
U.S. Navy, 26
University of Kentucky, 46
University of Maryland, 46
University of Michigan, 27
University of Nebraska at Omaha, 46
University of Pennsylvania, 27
University of Virginia, 27, 29
University-based programs, 26–28
Upward mobility, 6
"Urban 13," 56, 57

V

Vice-presidents
       participants, 37
       placement, 35
       professional development interests, 19
       seminars, 45
Vision: need for, 12, 15

W

Wabash College, 27
WACUBO (see Western Association of College and University Business Officers)
Wang, 22
Wang Institute of Graduate Studies, 29
Washington and Lee University, 27
Wellesley College, 40
Western Association of College and University Business Officers (WACUBO), 46, 69
Western Electric's Corporate Education Center, 26

ASHE-ERIC HIGHER EDUCATION REPORTS

Since 1983, the Association for the Study of Higher Education (ASHE) and the ERIC Clearinghouse on Higher Education at the George Washington University have cosponsored the ASHE-ERIC Higher Education Report series. The 1987 series is the sixteenth overall, with the American Association for Higher Education having served as cosponsor before 1983.

Each monograph is the definitive analysis of a tough higher education problem, based on thorough research of pertinent literature and institutional experiences. After topics are identified by a national survey, noted practitioners and scholars write the reports, with experts reviewing each manuscript before publication.

Eight monographs (10 monographs before 1985) in the ASHE-ERIC Higher Education Report series are published each year, available individually or by subscription. Subscription to eight issues is $60 regular; $50 for members of AERA, AAHE, and AIR; $40 for members of ASHE (add $7.50 for postage outside the United States).

Prices for single copies, including 4th class postage and handling, are $10.00 regular and $7.50 for members of AERA, AAHE, AIR, and ASHE ($7.50 regular and $6.00 for members for 1983 and 1984 reports, $6.50 regular and $5.00 for members for reports published before 1983). If faster 1st class postage is desired for U.S. and Canadian orders, add $.75 for each publication ordered; overseas, add $4.50. For VISA and MasterCard payments, include card number, expiration date, and signature. Orders under $25 must be prepaid. Bulk discounts are available on orders of 15 or more reports (not applicable to subscriptions). Order from the Publications Department, ASHE-ERIC Higher Education Reports, the George Washington University, One Dupont Circle, Suite 630, Washington, D.C. 20036-1183, or phone us at 202/296-2597. Write for a publication list of all the Higher Education Reports available.

1987 ASHE-ERIC Higher Education Reports

1. Incentive Early Retirement Programs for Faculty: Innovative Responses to a Changing Environment
   Jay L. Chronister and Thomas R. Kepple, Jr.

2. Working Effectively with Trustees: Building Cooperative Campus Leadership
   Barbara E. Taylor

3. Formal Recognition of Employer-Sponsored Instruction: Conflict and Collegiality in Postsecondary Education
   Nancy S. Nash and Elizabeth M. Hawthorne

4. Learning Styles: Implications for Improving Educational Practices
   Charles S. Claxton and Patricia H. Murrell

5. Higher Education Leadership: Enhancing Skills through Professional Development Programs
   Sharon A. McDade

1986 ASHE-ERIC Higher Education Reports

1. Post-tenure Faculty Evaluation: Threat or Opportunity?
   Christine M. Licata

2. Blue Ribbon Commissions and Higher Education: Changing Academe

from the Outside
Janet R. Johnson and Lawrence R. Marcus

3. Responsive Professional Education: Balancing Outcomes and Opportunities
Joan S. Stark, Malcolm A. Lowther, and Bonnie M.K. Hagerty

4. Increasing Students' Learning: A Faculty Guide to Reducing Stress among Students
Neal A. Whitman, David C. Spendlove, and Claire H. Clark

5. Student Financial Aid and Women: Equity Dilemma?
Mary Moran

6. The Master's Degree: Tradition, Diversity, Innovation
Judith S. Glazer

7. The College, the Constitution, and the Consumer Student: Implications for Policy and Practice
Robert M. Hendrickson and Annette Gibbs

8. Selecting College and University Personnel: The Quest and the Questions
Richard A. Kaplowitz

1985 ASHE-ERIC Higher Education Reports

1. Flexibility in Academic Staffing: Effective Policies and Practices
Kenneth P. Mortimer, Marque Bagshaw, and Andrew T. Masland

2. Associations in Action: The Washington, D.C., Higher Education Community
Harland G. Bloland

3. And on the Seventh Day: Faculty Consulting and Supplemental Income
Carol M. Boyer and Darrell R. Lewis

4. Faculty Research Performance: Lessons from the Sciences and Social Sciences
John W. Creswell

5. Academic Program Reviews: Institutional Approaches, Expectations, and Controversies
Clifton F. Conrad and Richard F. Wilson

6. Students in Urban Settings: Achieving the Baccalaureate Degree
Richard C. Richardson, Jr., and Louis W. Bender

7. Serving More Than Students: A Critical Need for College Student Personnel Services
Peter H. Garland

8. Faculty Participation in Decision Making: Necessity or Luxury?
Carol E. Floyd

1984 ASHE-ERIC Higher Education Reports

1. Adult Learning: State Policies and Institutional Practices
K. Patricia Cross and Anne-Marie McCartan

2. Student Stress: Effects and Solutions
Neal A. Whitman, David C. Spendlove, and Claire H. Clark

3. Part-time Faculty: Higher Education at a Crossroads
   Judith M. Gappa

4. Sex Discrimination Law in Higher Education: The Lessons of the Past Decade
   J. Ralph Lindgren, Patti T. Ota, Perry A. Zirkel, and Nan Van Gieson

5. Faculty Freedoms and Institutional Accountability: Interactions and Conflicts
   Steven G. Olswang and Barbara A. Lee

6. The High-Technology Connection: Academic/Industrial Cooperation for Economic Growth
   Lynn G. Johnson

7. Employee Educational Programs: Implications for Industry and Higher Education
   Suzanne W. Morse

8. Academic Libraries: The Changing Knowledge Centers of Colleges and Universities
   Barbara B. Moran

9. Futures Research and the Strategic Planning Process: Implications for Higher Education
   James L. Morrison, William L. Renfro, and Wayne I. Boucher

10. Faculty Workload: Research, Theory, and Interpretation
    Harold E. Yuker

1983 ASHE-ERIC Higher Education Reports

1. The Path to Excellence: Quality Assurance in Higher Education
   Laurence R. Marcus, Anita O. Leone, and Edward D. Goldberg

2. Faculty Recruitment, Retention, and Fair Employment: Obligations and Opportunities
   John S. Waggaman

3. Meeting the Challenges: Developing Faculty Careers
   Michael C.T. Brookes and Katherine L. German

4. Raising Academic Standards: A Guide to Learning Improvement
   Ruth Talbott Keimig

5. Serving Learners at a Distance: A Guide to Program Practices
   Charles E. Feasley

6. Competence, Admissions, and Articulation: Returning to the Basics in Higher Education
   Jean L. Preer

7. Public Service in Higher Education: Practices and Priorities
   Patricia H. Crosson

8. Academic Employment and Retrenchment: Judicial Review and Administrative Action
   Robert M. Hendrickson and Barbara A. Lee

9. Burnout: The New Academic Disease*
   Winifred Albizu Meléndez and Rafael M. de Guzmán

10. Academic Workplace: New Demands, Heightened Tensions
    Ann E. Austin and Zelda F. Gamson

*Out-of-print. Available through EDRS.

Dear Educator,

I welcome the ASHE-ERIC monograph series. The series is a service to those who need brief but dependable analyses of key issues in higher education.
(Rev.) Theodore M. Hesburgh, C.S.C.
President Emeritus, University of Notre Dame

Order Form

Quantity   Amount

_____ Please enter my subscription to the 1987 ASHE-ERIC
Higher Education Reports at $60.00, 25% off the cover
price ($40.00 ASHE members).   _____

_____ Please enter my subscription to the 1988 Higher Edu- _____
cation Reports at $60.00 ($40.00 ASHE members).

_____ Outside U.S., add $7.50 for postage per series.   _____

Individual reports are available at the following prices:
1985 and forward, $10.00 each ($7.50 for ASHE members).
1983 and 1984, $7.50 each ($6.00 for ASHE members).
1982 and back, $6.50 each ($5.00 for ASHE members).

Please send me the following reports:

_____ Report No. ___ (_____)   _____
_____ Report No. ___ (_____)   _____
_____ Report No. ___ (_____)   _____

SUBTOTAL: _____
Optional 1st Class Shipping ($.75 per book) _____
TOTAL AMOUNT DUE: _____

NOTE: All prices subject to change.

Name _____

Title _____

Institution _____

Address _____

_____

City _____ State _____ ZIP _____

Phone _____

Signature _____
☐ Check enclosed, payable to ASHE.
☐ Please charge my credit card:
                ☐ VISA   ☐ MasterCard (check one)

Expiration date _____

Send to: ASHE-ERIC Higher Education Reports
The George Washington University
One Dupont Circle, Suite 630, Dept. G4
Washington, D.C. 20036-1183